MY STRUGGLE FOR FREEDOM

BY JOSEF NOVÁK

(based on **VZPOMÍNKY VETERÁNA**)

MELANDRIUM BOOKS

Published by
MELANDRIUM BOOKS
11 Highway Lane
Keele
Staffs ST5 5AN

© Josef Novák

All rights reserved. No part of this publication may be reproduced or transmitted in any form or by any means, electronic or mechanical including photocopying, recording or any information storage or retrieval system, without prior permission in writing from the publishers.

First published 2010
Reprinted 2012
ISBN No. 0-9537853-7-8

Designed by **MELANDRIUM BOOKS**
and printed in England by Keele Graphic Services.
Reprinted by The Book Factory, Stoke-on-Trent.

MELANDRIUM BOOKS is proud to publish this book by Josef Novák in English on behalf of Československá Obec Legionářská v zahraničí (The Association of Czechoslovak Legionaries Abroad) on the occasion of the 70th Anniversary of the arrival of the Czechoslovak Voluntary Forces in the United Kingdom in July 1940. It is based on his book **Vypomínky veterána** which was published by the Univerzita Palackého v Olomouci in 2009.

It is a remarkable story of a man who fought against oppression and sought freedom. During the Second World War he was obliged to join the Wehrmacht on the Eastern Front. When he was sent back to Germany with frostbite he contrived to join the Western Front and then escaped to join the Allied Forces. For his valour under fire he was awarded the Military Medal by King George VI.

After the War he returned to Czechoslovakia; but following the Communist *coup* in 1948 he was sentenced to 16 years' imprisonment by the Communist regime. He escaped once more, to freedom in England, and became a very successful business man.

In this book he poses the question:
"Where is my homeland?"

This book is sold in aid of
Československá Obec Legionářská v zahraničí

Dedication

This book is dedicated to my children, my grandchildren, my great-grandchildren and to my comrades-in-arms.

I also wish to thank Richard Northern for all his helpful suggestions, and John Kolbert without whose help this book would not have been published in English.

Josef Novák

Gallantry Medals

Military Medal   **Czechoslovak War Cross**   **For Bravery**   **Czechoslovak Army Medal**

Campaign Medals

Contents

Chapter 1	Early Years in Czechoslovakia	1
Chapter 2	In Bondage to the Poles	16
Chapter 3	German Occupation	23
Chapter 4	Forced to join the Wehrmacht	28
Chapter 5	Move to Russia	37
Chapter 6	Sent Back Home	47
Chapter 7	Back to France	53
Chapter 8	Five Minutes to Midnight	64
Chapter 9	The Battle for Dunkirk	70
Chapter 10	The Disappointment of the Liberation of the Homeland	87
Chapter 11	Five Minutes to Midnight - the second time	95
Chapter 12	Hard Times in England	102
Chapter 13	The Fruits of Honest Labour	108
Chapter 14	Back Home after 20 Years	115
Chapter 15	At Home in England	121
Chapter 16	The Joy of 1989	123
Appendix		

MY STRUGGLE FOR FREEDOM

Chapter 1: Early Years in Czechoslovakia

I was born in Těšin, a small town in Silesia. For more than a thousand years this part of North Eastern Moravia near the Polish border has been a source of conflict, sovereignty being contested by Poland, Hungary, Prussia and Bohemia. During the late-eighteenth century it became generally attached to Bohemia and then, by inheritance, to the Austrian Hapsburgs. Through the centuries many immigrants from Germany had settled in the area, alongside the Poles and Czechs already living there, and they too laid claim to the province.

In 1918, at the end of the First World War, this caused many problems between the newly formed state of Czechoslovakia and Poland. The Poles claimed all the land east of Ostrava but the Czechs claimed all land west of Skoczow. To put an end to this conflict and avoid another war, a plebiscite was arranged in 1920 to enable the people to choose to which country the region should belong. The result was indecisive and Silesia was divided between the two. The river Olza, flowing through the centre of our town, was the dividing line between Polish Těšin and Czech Těšin. The idea was that the Czechs would move to Czechoslovakia on the western side of the river and the Poles to Poland on the eastern side, but though most Czechs were leaving Poland many Polish people refused to leave Czechoslovakia.

When I was born in March 1923, because of the difficulty in finding accommodation in Czech Těšin, my parents were living with my paternal grandparents in Polish Těšin, where they and their three children (Leoš, Emilie and Marie) had one small room. With another baby it was no longer possible for the family to manage in this confined space, but my father was lucky enough to find a little house to rent on the Czech side of the river. This consisted of one large room and a kitchen, where there was a large table, around which we could all sit, and a bed. The lavatory was outside, as was the well which provided our water supply. The main advantage was that my father could walk to work in only ten minutes instead of the one-and-a-half hours it had taken when we lived in Polish Těšin.

My brother Rudolf was born in January 1925 and within a year my mother was expecting another child, so once again Father had to look for a larger house. This he found in the small village of Ropice, the next railway station up the line from Český Těšin. Our new house had two bedrooms and a kitchen, where we ate our meals and which was also used as a living-room. The following October my sister Anna was born. Altogether we were nine – parents, three boys, three girls and a grandmother who was given a home by my parents when she had nowhere to live.

In 1928, when I was five years old, I started at the Infants' School. I was always eager to learn and found lessons very enjoyable. When I moved to Primary School a year later I encountered a situation which was difficult for a six year old to understand. Our school was divided into two parts – one half Czech, where I was a pupil, and the other Polish, which a friend I played with every day attended. On the first day I walked to school with him in the morning but after school, when I saw him chatting to a group of boys and went to join them, he told me to go away because I did not belong with them. I could not understand what was happening. My father explained that some Polish people, who did not accept the results of the plebiscite held at the end of the World War, were still creating problems.

When I asked our teacher why the Poles were so unfriendly and claimed that the land where we lived belonged to them he told us that, as citizens of a democratic state, we must live in friendship and peace with minority groups. I could not understand why I had to behave in a friendly fashion when Polish people were so hostile. Father told me not to worry because we would soon be moving from Ropice to the village of Mosty, where I would find new friends. He had found a piece of land where we could build a bigger house with plenty of room for everybody. As a State employee he was able to get a bank loan to buy the land from a farmer, who was offering plots to people willing to help him by working in his fields or on the farm at harvest time.

Several families were building houses and my father had picked a plot with a large garden at the end of the lane by the edge of the forest. It was a beautiful place – a paradise for us children. Throughout our youth we practically lived in the woods. Father built the house himself with the help of a few craftsmen. He spent every Saturday and Sunday on the site and I always went with him. I enjoyed being there but though I always wanted to help I was usually in the way. To keep me happy they would give me some small job, such as collecting timber to make a fire to warm our meals.

I was seven years old when my youngest sister, Eliška, was born soon after we moved into our new home in 1930. Here we had four rooms, as well as an attic and a cellar, which was used to store food. There were ten of us now, but there was enough room for everyone. In the beginning we drew our water from a well in the garden – a large plot, where we could grow vegetables. Life here was very pleasant. Every morning we were awakened by birdsong. Ruda and I made new friends in the village – boys in those days tended to stick together. In the woods we discovered many different animals and plants – there was something new and exciting every day. Our little house by the forest was like a fairytale.

Father was still working on the railway and, like most women in those days, Mother looked after the house and garden. Being so young I did not realise now how hard it must have been for her cleaning, washing (no vacuum cleaners or washing machines in those days) and cooking for a family of ten, as well as tending the garden. All the vegetables we ate were home grown. Besides her work at home, in the summer she helped in the fields belonging to our local farmer.

My stepbrother Leoš was ten years older than me. When he left school at the age of fourteen he was apprenticed to a painter and decorator. He completed his apprenticeship after three years but was then laid off. As an apprentice he received no wages, but once he had served his time his employer could not afford to pay him a tradesman's rate. There was little demand for this type of work and few jobs were available. In Silesia most jobs were in coalmining and the iron and steel industry. Leoš was very disappointed - he had hoped that after finishing his apprenticeship he would be able to earn a living as a decorator. He decided to stay in the trade for which he had trained and started his own small business, even though he had to work for very low rates if he wanted to attract customers.

When I was eight I did something of which I was ashamed. One day, passing a sweetshop, where the owner was decorating his window with Christmas sweets, I quickly slipped a chocolate Saint Nicholas into my pocket when he turned away for a second. I did not take this for myself; I wanted to put it on our Christmas tree, for which we had only homemade decorations. We would cut out and colour paper stars and animals to hang on the tree, along with chains we made from scrap paper. The little Saint Nicholas was wrapped in colourful foil and I thought it would look beautiful. I showed this to my sister, Emilie, but when she told our father I had to explain to him how I got it. I had never seen him so angry. He took off his belt and gave me a good hiding, telling me that being poor did not give us the right to steal anything we wanted. He gave me one crown and sent me back to the shop. I had to give back the chocolate and pay for it because, after being in my pocket, it no longer looked new. I walked around the shop for about quarter of an hour before I plucked up the courage to go in. I explained to the shopkeeper what I had done and gave him the chocolate and the money. "Now that you have paid for it you can keep it", he said. "I dare not disobey my father's orders", I told him sadly, putting the chocolate on the counter and quickly walking away. Later I heard my father telling my mother that the shopkeeper had stopped him on his way home from work, and had told him that, if all parents were like him, we would not need any policemen.

Along with Leoš, Emilie and Marie, I was a member of our local Sokol Club, a patriotic and non-political gymnastic association. Leoš was very disappointed in me and reminded me that members of Sokol must always act responsibly so as not to give the organization a bad name. I felt very guilty and promised never to do anything like this again. He told me that no one could have something for nothing; what one wanted one must pay for. As he was self-employed, he asked if I would like to earn a few crowns by helping him. I was happy to do this because I wanted to atone for what I had done and I was trying to save some money for a trip to the mountains in the summer. The work was not difficult. Usually I took his equipment on my little handcart to and from wherever he was working. My other job was mixing paint – in those days the decorator prepared his own. I mixed the white powder, and colour if required, with water, making sure it was thoroughly dissolved. I used to do this after school and during the holidays.

All young men had to complete two years National Service in the Army. When Leoš returned to civilian life he joined the police force. Emilie, who suffered from asthma, stayed at home once she had finished her schooling, to help my mother. Marie was lucky to get an unpaid apprenticeship to a hairdresser, for which Father had to pay a fee of fifty crowns per month.

About a year later I was running to school because I was late, when a man stepped from a car a few hundred metres ahead of me and walked away across the fields towards a farm. As I ran past I noticed a wallet lying by the car. It was stuffed with money and as there was no one else around I knew it must belong to this man. When I ran after him and asked if it were his, he realised his breast pocket was empty. He was very relieved and thanked me profusely. I told him I must hurry as I was already late for school, but he offered me a lift in his car. I was thrilled because I had never ridden in a car before. It was a very comfortable drive and my school friends were very surprised to see me get out. The gentleman went to tell the teacher what had happened and asked if I could be excused school for the day – he wanted to reward me for my honesty. I was very proud when the teacher praised me before the whole class. I was excused from school but only my parents could give permission for me to visit his house. My father was at work but when my mother heard what had happened she agreed that I could go to spend the day playing with his son.

He lived in Český Těšin in a beautiful house with a large garden. His son, Zdeněk, who was about my age, was not very well. I do not know what was wrong with him but he was very weak and spent most of the time sitting around. He was very happy to have someone to play with. There was a swing in the garden; he had a bicycle and more toys than I ever knew existed. To me this was heaven. His mother brought us chocolate, toffees, fruit and cake, with juice to drink. I did not know which to try first. We started to play football – he was so happy, running about and laughing all the time, but his mother came out and told us he must not run. When I was leaving he asked me if I would like to come to play with him again. I had been to play with him a couple of times when his mother asked me not to call again as he was very tired and unwell. I felt sorry for him, leading such a lonely and friendless life. My father was pleased with me and pointed out that honesty always pays. Some seven hundred people lived in Mosty, and the news soon spread round the village. I was proud that I had done something to give our family a good name.

At harvest time when my mother was working in the fields for the farmer from whom we had bought our plot of land, I too helped on the farm and ran errands for him. Once my reward was a little pig – I carried it in a sack over my shoulder and it squealed all the way home. My mother was delighted and father promised that we would make a nice big pig out of him. All our food scraps went to feed him and I used to get quite excited when I checked how much he had grown.

I was happy to go to school, except for one thing. As in Ropice, the school was divided into Polish and Czech sections; there were always problems between the children from both sides. We in the Czech school were taught that in a democratic state minority groups had the same rights we had, and that we should live in friendship and peace with everyone. In the Polish school it was quite different; there they were taught that we Czechs were their enemies and that Silesia belonged to Poland. I found this difficult to understand. We were taught to set an example in good manners and to greet people in the street with a polite "Good morning." I was puzzled that the Poles did not reply when I spoke to them. The situation was even worse with the Germans, who would speak only their own language and answer with a brusque "Grüss Gott." When we complained about this our teacher explained that everyone had the right to speak whatever language they chose. I still could not understand why, if they hated us so much, they did not return to their own countries, which they liked so much better. Again we were told that Czechoslovakia was a democratic state, where we must live in harmony with the Poles and the Germans, even if they would not speak our language. I did not agree with this – I felt that if they wanted to live in our country they should integrate with us. Eventually I sorted things in my own way – if someone ignored my Czech greeting I did not greet them again.

In school I usually had good results in exams but when we started to learn German my worst mark was always in that subject. The antagonism shown by Poles and Germans caused Czechs to band more closely together, even though at the time we had no idea of the danger we could expect from these people in the future. I was a very keen member of the local Sokol Club, where we practised gymnastics. I was happy that all the members were Czech and very patriotic, but to the Poles and Germans we were bitter enemies. Whenever we arranged any kind of show, a play or a dance, the Poles would try to disrupt our plans but we would not let them succeed. We simply drew closer together in the face of this hostility.

When I was eleven I moved to Secondary School in Český Těšin, where I made a lot of new friends. I was thrilled when they invited me to join them on a Scout trip to the forest. This was a very interesting experience but I soon realised that boys who lived in the town had no idea about the countryside, where I felt most at home. We were divided into two groups, each group having to erect a tent and cook a meal. All my friends wore scout uniform – I was the only one without, as my parents could not afford to buy me one. I had to keep my white shirt and short trousers clean for school the next day. This was the only shirt I had so, to avoid getting it dirty, I took it off, placed it, with my trousers and shoes in a neat pile, and wore only my boxer shorts. The other boys had no idea why I needed to keep my clothes clean.

Once the tents were up we went to collect the wood for our fire. I knew the kind of wood to collect – dry twigs lying on the ground, which were very easy to break into small pieces. We soon had our fire burning nicely but the other group was not so successful. Instead of looking for dry twigs they gathered newly cut branches, which were still green; they could not break them and when they finally got their fire going there was a lot of smoke but no flames. Before we set out it was arranged that each boy would bring with him an item of food. Each group would pool their resources and use them to cook a meal, after which we would play games. The kind of food was not specified; I think it was a test by the leader to see how we would cope with that problem. When my group took out their food it was catastrophic. They had brought rolls with salami, cakes, chocolate, sausages and fruit from which it was impossible to prepare a cooked meal. As I had no idea what we wanted to cook I had asked my mother for advice and she suggested that the easiest thing would be to make potato soup. I had no idea what the other boys would bring, but she had given me a few potatoes, an onion, a piece of bacon, a couple of eggs and a little flour and salt and told me that if I could find a few mushrooms in the woods I could use them too. I also took a small chopping board, a knife and a pan. When I took out my stuff everyone wondered what I would do with it. I peeled and cubed my six large potatoes, and put them into a pot hanging on a tripod over the fire; in the small pan I cooked the bacon and onion, cut into very small pieces, before adding flour. When this was brown I poured in some water, brought it to the boil and added it to the potatoes with a little salt and the two beaten eggs, along with some chopped salami from one of the other boys. The only snag with the potato soup was that there was not much of it and when all the other boys had had some there was none left for me. That didn't matter – I was happy that it tasted good and everybody liked it. We shared the rest of the food the others had brought, so no one went hungry. The second group finally brought some dry wood to get their fire going but they had only sausages.

After dinner, we sat round the fire and our leader pointed out the mistakes we had made. He said that first each group should have chosen a leader and decided beforehand what they would cook and what food each boy should bring. It was important to have dry wood for the fire, even though it took more time to find. He cited me as an example and told them that they should learn from me because I was always ready to do any kind of job. His praise did not help me because I could see from their faces that the other boys did not like this very much, and I felt unhappy. I was not used to being praised.

In the afternoon we played games, one of which was to teach us how to use the terrain. Six little flags were put on the edge of the woods near our camp, always near some bushes or flowers. The idea was that one group would watch the flags from a distance of about ten metres and the second group would try to steal the flags without being seen. My group was the first to try to capture the flags while the other group was guarding them. I had played this kind of game many times with my friends in Mosty; I knew it was important to camouflage ourselves, to be able to crawl quietly and to be patient. We had succeeded in taking four of the flags but one was in a very difficult place to reach. Two of our boys were detected as they tried to take it and were eliminated from the game. After some discussion it was decided that I should try. I was more than willing but pointed out that I would need help. I asked one boy to hide behind a nearby bush where there was no flag; when I gave him a sign he should shake the bush to distract the guard. Wearing only shorts, covered in mud and a few leaves, I was well camouflaged and came within a metre of the target. The boy behind me passed on my signal to the decoy, who started to shake the bush. As soon as the watchers looked in his direction I brought into play a hook I had made from a small branch; when they looked back the flag was gone. Later, when it was our turn to guard the flags, I warned that we must not take our eyes from the flags, no matter what happened. We captured five flags but our vigilance paid off as our opponents managed to take only one. After the game I washed in the stream, and put on my clean clothes; the dirty boxers went into my rucksack. The boys who had worn their uniforms all day were filthy but happy; they had enjoyed our games in the countryside very much. This trip was one of the happiest days of my youth. Some friends from my group invited me to become a permanent member of the troop.

On the way back the group leader asked how I had enjoyed the outing and he, too, asked if I would like to become a member of his scout troop. I was shy and did not know how to explain. In the end I plucked up my courage and told him that I would like to but could not; because we were ten in the family and very poor my parents could not afford to buy me a uniform and if we were to go for another trip they could not give me any money. After some thought he told me he had been watching me all day and realised I had potential; I had dealt capably with several problems and I made friends quickly, which was important for any leader. I did not understand what he meant or what to say. He suggested that he could help me start a scout group with my friends in Mosty.

When I mentioned this to my friends in Sokol they were very enthusiastic and we started our own troop under the leadership of Český Těšin. We began with six members; later we were nine. In summer we met in the woods and in winter in the gym. Later, the parents of one our members allowed us to use an empty room in their house as our clubroom. I was elected leader of the group. We had a varied programme, but spent most of our time in the woods. We learnt to communicate by semaphore and Morse code; we practised tracking each other, map-reading, first-aid, protecting the woods and the wildlife. The only thing missing was a uniform. At our meetings this was a regular topic of discussion and we decided that a shirt would be enough for us, but the problem was how to raise money for this.

Our leader from Český Těšín was always ready to help us, and suggested that we should organize a "lucky dip" at the school Open Day. We explained what we wanted to do to the School Director, who gladly gave his permission. We decided that we would use a piece of cloth about one and a half metres high to screen off the area where we could place our prizes; outside we would sell numbered tickets, which would then be hooked on to a fishing rod. These the buyers would cast over the screen, where we would attach to the hook the prize corresponding to the ticket number and the "fisherman" would reel it in. Our biggest problem was to find the prizes. We went round the local shopkeepers, who donated toys, pens, pencils and stationery, but we still did not have enough and decided we must make a few more prizes ourselves. One shopkeeper gave us some old photographic plates he was throwing away and told us that if we washed them we would have clean pieces of glass the size of a postcard. We collected postcards from holidays, put them behind the glass and taped round the edges to make pictures. We had about 250 prizes and sold the tickets for 1 crown. After deducting our expenses we had 230 crowns.

When we went to buy the material for our uniforms we realised we still did not have enough money but, after explaining why we needed it, one of the shopkeepers gave us some discount. The mother of one of our boys was a dressmaker, and she agreed to make the shirts for us. Although we had no money we offered to pay her in kind – we would help in her garden and the field where she grew potatoes and cabbages. She made our shirts and we kept our promise to work for her. We were so happy when we could wear our uniform – and very proud that we had managed this by our own efforts.

In the woods where we met there was a dilapidated wooden hut in an abandoned sand quarry. The quarry owner accepted our offer to repair the hut if he would allow us to use it as a meeting place. We usually met on Sunday and one day we had a visit from the forester who looked after the woods belonging to the State. He had seen the smoke from our fire, which is forbidden in the woods, and came to investigate. We told him we were Scouts and assured him that we understood the danger. This was why the fire was in the quarry where there was only sand, and no wood or bushes. We had built it within a circle of stones, and a bucket of water was at hand in case of emergency. Before we left we always made sure the fire was out. He was pleased with our precautions. He stayed for a while and told us stories about the animals living in the woods and the protection they needed. After this he often met us and talked to us about the World War. He had been wounded during the fighting and because of this had been given his job as forester. He loved the woods and the animals living there, and taught us a lot about animal life. He was happy that we were interested in country life and he told us that as Scouts we could help him to protect the environment against people who sometimes unintentionally did a lot of damage. When they came to picnic on Sundays noisy children could disturb the animals, frightening them away from the woods, and they often broke the newly planted trees. We promised to help him and started straight away with this work.

On Sundays we were always watching. When we saw families coming into the woods we would start a friendly conversation and explain to the children that this was home to the little animals and birds. We asked them to play quietly so that these small creatures were not frightened and to be careful not to break the small trees. It was interesting to see how quietly they would sit and listen to us. Our forester had told us that most children love animals. I always offered to bring fresh water from our house, which was just at the edge of the forest. I would bring the parents a jug of cold water with some homemade raspberry juice and some strawberries from the garden for the children. The children were happy and the parents were grateful; when they asked what I wanted for this service I always told them it was up to them whether they wanted to give anything or not. I mentioned that our group was saving for a trip to the mountains, and sometimes they would give me a couple of crowns. I would bring a jugful of water for any visitor to the woods and more often than not I would be given a crown. In this way I saved enough money for our troop to make a trip to the Beskydy Mountains.

At the beginning of July, when our school holidays began, we set off for the mountains on foot as we did not have enough money for the train. We started at a mountain called Ropicka in the Beskydy, from where we went along the ridge to the next mountain and finished on Velký Polom. Our supplies of food were running low and the money we had saved was already gone; the few crowns we had left were needed to buy food for the journey home. When we went to buy bread at the tourist hotel we met a gentleman from our village, who knew us all well. Mr. Vallach was on a two-week holiday and asked what we were doing there. We told him we were camping but had to go back home because we had used up all our money. He mentioned that on the next day there would be a celebration to commemorate the martyrdom of Jan Hus. Jan Hus was a Master at Prague University and a popular preacher at the Bethlehem Chapel in the Old Town in Prague. He came into conflict with the Catholic Church when he supported the teachings of the English thinker, John Wycliffe who professed that the Church should be carrying out its primary pastoral mission instead of acquiring wealth and wielding political influence. In 1414, when Hus attended the Ecclesiastical Council in Constance, he was arrested soon after his arrival and charged with heresy. He refused to recant and on 6th July 1415 was burned at the stake as a heretic. His followers, the Hussites, revered him as a martyr, and as children we always looked forward to the bonfire lit in his memory. Mr. Vallach asked if we would like to help to build the big bonfire for the celebration. Afterwards, wearing our uniforms, we should make a ring round the fire and at the end of the formal speeches we should step forward, saying very loudly the words: "Český Těšín greets Prague, Brno and all the guests on Polom." We were happy to do this and after the celebrations ended we went back to our tent, made a small fire and started singing. One of my friends,

Pepík, had a beautiful voice so it was easy to join in. Mr. Vallach came to tell us the guests in the hotel from Prague and Brno had liked our greeting very much and they were giving us 50 crowns. We were delighted. Many of the visitors, attracted by our singing, came to our fire and sang along with us till late into the night. Next day two of our scouts went down the mountain to buy food in the village so that we could stay another week. In the evenings we would sit round the fire, the guests from the hotel would join us and usually we finished with more and more songs. It was a beautiful holiday in the Beskydy.

I was fourteen years old in 1937 and would have liked to continue in school. I was very interested in engineering but my parents could not afford to finance this. Because further schooling was out of the question I wanted to become an apprentice auto-mechanic but soon realised how difficult it was to get into this type of work. As most businesses in Silesia were owned by Germans the first requirement was to be fluent in German, and the few words I had learnt in school were not enough. I hated the language and was always the bottom of the class in this subject. In the end I was taken on as an apprentice tailor in a small business employing three qualified tailors and three apprentices. The owner, although Jewish, considered himself to be German. He spoke German to his customers but, because he spoke Czech very badly, he usually asked me to fill in all his papers when necessary. He was an interesting person, born on the 8th August, 1888. Because his birthday numbers were all eights he considered them to be his lucky numbers. He believed that if the Nazis were to take over our country he would be safe because he was German. How wrong he was. A few years earlier he had been on his way to America. He was already on a ship in Hamburg when he decided to come back to Czechoslovakia because he liked it so much. Poor man! He did not know what the future held in store for him. I was a very quick learner and was one of his favourites. My hours were from 7am till 6pm on weekdays and on Saturday from 7 am till 2pm. Our boss did not work on Saturday, the Jewish Sabbath, even though the shop was open.

That summer the Sokol Organization held a festival in Prague. I was fourteen years old, still a very keen member of our club, and I wanted to go to this. As usual, the problem was that I did not have the money for the fare. My parents could not help me – they too had no money to finance this trip. The local branch decided to pay for two teenage members to attend this event. When they told me that I had been selected I was over the moon. I could not wait for the day to come. For me it was an unforgettable experience. We travelled on a goods train, which I did not mind at all – the only thing that mattered was that I was going to Prague. The train was packed with happy people and the atmosphere was terrific. We passed the time singing patriotic songs, such as: "We won't give up Prague, We would rather raze it to the ground" and "Don't wait for us, Hitler. You will never get us. When the bombs fall from the sky you'll get one as well". We were all ready, young as we were, to protect our homeland and I was very proud to be one of them.

I enjoyed my time in Prague. I wore a uniform lent to me by the Těšin branch of Sokol. We spent every possible minute proudly walking through the streets, especially in Wenceslas Square. The few days of this festival were for me the best days in my life. At that time I had no idea what was waiting for me in the future.

Chapter 2: In Bondage to the Poles

After our return from Prague the situation in Silesia went from bad to worse. Radio Katowice was constantly broadcasting propaganda from Poland, claiming that the Poles living in Czechoslovakia were being victimized, which was quite untrue, and that Silesia belonged to Poland.

The Government began to build concrete bunkers along the borders to protect our country against attack and a blackout was imposed. Because many Polish families ignored this ruling we, as members of Sokol, volunteered to patrol our village to make sure that these regulations were observed. When some of our patrols were attacked we began to work in fours and carried sticks for protection.

In the late summer of 1938 the soldiers in the concrete bunkers started packing, ready to leave. When I asked them why, I was told that they were obeying orders. I was very upset because I thought that they were there to resist the Poles if they tried to invade our country. Soldiers were leaving the nearby barracks as well and we felt that we were being abandoned. On 1st October crowds gathered in Český Těšin at the bridge over the River Olza where the border crossing was located. I went to see what was going on, astonished to hear that Silesia was being handed over to Poland. I did not want to believe this and tried to get closer to the front of the crowd to find out if it was indeed true. As I came nearer to the checkpoint I saw Czech and Polish officers standing there. The Czech officer handed papers to the Pole, with these words: "To-day us; tomorrow you. You will not enjoy a year here." Future events proved these words were prophetic. Eleven months later Silesia was occupied as the German army invaded Poland. I still could not understand why we gave Silesia to Poland without a fight. Because we had no radio at home and could not afford to buy a newspaper we had no idea what was happening in the outside world.

To me the Poles were the enemy but, in reality, our main enemy was Germany. It was only later that we got to know about the appeasement policy towards Hitler by Britain, France and Italy. This culminated in the Munich Agreement. Czechoslovakia had no representation, yet the Agreement sanctioned the annexation of the Sudetenland into Germany, and at the same time Hungary occupied part of Slovakia. We were attacked from three sides and were helped by no one. The following days in our region were very difficult. Poles were harming Czechs whenever they could. In our village they threw granite through the window of a Czech house; it was lucky that there was no one in the sitting-room at the time. Shops were closed and the goods taken away to Poland.

One day Father arrived home from work slightly tipsy. The workers on the railway had received only a small deposit on their wages, so he went with friends to the pub to discuss the situation. What annoyed them most was that instead of money they were given a Polish cap, decorated with a Polish eagle. Unhappy and angry, they drank more than they should. When he came home he threw the cap on the floor and started jumping on it till it was ruined, declaring angrily: "Instead of money they gave us a stupid chicken. I'd like to wring its neck." He thought of the eagle on his hat as a chicken. Next day he was sorry, because his cap was completely useless and he had to wear the old Czech one. When asked why he was not wearing the Polish cap, the point being made that he was now a Pole living in Poland, he told them that he had not received one. Because no signature had been requested when the cap was issued, they could not prove him wrong. He was given another and was compelled to wear it.

One Sunday my younger brother and I were walking along the main road on the way home from church when we had to pass a group of Poles and Polish soldiers. As we walked by a local person in the group called out: "Get them. They are Czechophiles." They started to chase us but we did not wait. When we saw more of them on the road we ran into the woods where there were some dangerous marshes. We were always warned to keep away from that part of the woods but on that day we had no choice: it was the forest and the marsh or a beating from the people who were chasing us. We were very lucky to get through safely and arrived home filthy. When we told our parents what had happened they forbade us to go to the church or into town until the situation improved.

There were soldiers, often drunk, everywhere. There were cases of them harassing women, some of whom were raped. One such case happened in woods near our house. I was sitting with friends at the edge of the forest, discussing the Polish occupation and our future, when we heard someone screaming for help. We ran in the direction of the noise and came upon a Polish soldier raping a young girl only twelve or thirteen years old. As we ran towards him, we saw his gun standing next to a tree about two metres away, but he was too drunk to get up quickly. My friend grabbed the gun and ran away with it. The soldier tried to follow him but couldn't walk straight and kept falling down. As soon as they were far enough away from the girl we took her to my home because it was the nearest. She was bleeding and all her body was shaking. My mother and sisters took her inside to try to calm her down and to stop the blood. Father sent me to bring her parents, who lived on the other side of the woods. She had been taking a short cut on her way home when the man had grabbed her. Her parents were grateful for our intervention. She was taken to hospital, where she stayed for quite a long time. When she returned home she was afraid of people and did not want to leave the house. The boy who had grabbed the gun told us that when he had eventually thrown it into the bushes the soldier, who had been following him, had rushed to retrieve it. The girl's parents reported this outrage to the Army command post but there they did not even want to talk to them.

My sisters were forbidden to go through the woods alone and they went everywhere in groups. When I was walking home from work about two months after the Polish occupation I ran into my friend Milan, who had formerly been an official of our Sokol Club. He originally came from Central Moravia and had had to escape with his family before the local Poles could get him. The pub he owned had been confiscated. He had come back secretly to find out what had happened to his property, but he was afraid he would be recognized and imprisoned. He and his family were living in a refugee camp at the time at a school in Frýdek Místek until he could find work and his own accommodation. I complained about the way we were being treated by the Poles and he told me that in his camp were a lot of young escapees. It was the late autumn of 1938 and I was fifteen years old. I was taking life under the Polish occupation very hard and decided I would go to join the Czechs who were living in Moravia. On Saturday I told only my mother, because my father was at work, that I was going to Ostrava to visit my stepbrother, Leoš; we had had no news from him for a long time. She agreed to my visit but was worried about how I would get past the Polish army guards. I went without luggage, taking only a sandwich, and set off for Frýdek Místek some thirty kilometres away. I was not sure exactly where the border was but, after walking for about four hours, I saw a crossroads where Polish soldiers were checking the people who went past. I thought this must be the checkpoint and started planning how to get through. The road led uphill and ahead I could see a small four-wheeled cart carrying hay. The man in front was pulling the cart and at the back a woman was pushing. Because of the gradient it was very hard work for them. Seeing a chance to get past the soldiers, I ran to help them. The soldiers took no notice of us as we passed. At the top of the hill we stopped, and they both thanked me for my help. I asked the lady where the border was and she pointed out a farmhouse by the road and told me that the line ran through the woods beyond the house. When she asked me if I wanted to get to the other side I said nothing, but she told me to watch out for patrols, which sometimes rested inside the farmhouse. They both wished me good luck and went on their way. Next to the farm was a field with piles of hay and as I was considering how I could get to the woods I saw two soldiers walking from the farm towards me. I quickly sat on the grass by the road, and started to eat my sandwich.

"Good Day," I said in Polish as they passed me. "You'd better get to work so the farmer doesn't see you doing nothing", one of them remarked. "I'm going! I'm going!" I answered. I grabbed a fork lying on the ground and began trying to pile the hay. The soldiers were laughing but I saw my chance and went from one pile to the next in the direction of the woods. When I came to the end of the field I stuck the fork in one of the haycocks, went forward slowly and stopped by the first tree, pretending that I was relieving myself in case someone was watching. I went a bit deeper into the wood - there were only a few trees, and I was soon on the other side.

After crossing another field I found myself back on the main road leading to Frýdek Místek. I reached the town in the early evening, happy to be on Czech soil again. It was not difficult to find the school, which was crowded. I soon located Milan, who helped me to find a place to sleep. He told me that the next day I would have to go to the office to register but warned me that I must tell them that I was eighteen years old or they would not accept me. After eating some soup I fell asleep.

Next day I went to register and when asked my name and date of birth. I replied very quickly that I was Josef Novák, born 11th March 1923. The man in the office looked at me. "Back to your mother, boy!" he said. "We can't take kids here." I realised with a shock that I had completely forgotten to change the year of my birth. Crestfallen, I went back to my room and told Milan what had happened and asked if he could lend me a few crowns so that I could go to my brother in Ostrava. Perhaps he would be able to help me so that I would not need to go back to Poland. I left immediately and arrived in Ostrava the same evening. Leoš was out but when I explained to his landlady that he was my brother she let me wait for him in his room. When he came home from work he was very surprised to see me. I explained what had happened and asked if I could stay with him as life under the Poles was unbearable. He told me he would be glad to have me but, as a policeman, he was forbidden to take in anyone born in Silesia and he dared not ignore a direct order. Only people born in the middle of the Republic, who were in Silesia as employees, were allowed entry. I was left with no alternative but to go back home. This was a bitter blow and very hard for me to accept.

I stayed with him for a few days and then, thoroughly dejected, left for home. I went back the way I had come. I stopped in Frýdek Místek to repay the money Milan had lent me. I asked again if there were any chance I could stay in Czechoslovakia, only to be told that the situation was deteriorating and that there was a lot of dangerous news coming from Germany. It looked like the Third Reich would soon occupy the rest of the Republic and a lot of young men were already escaping beyond the border via Poland. His advice was that it would be better for me to stay in Poland and not to forget that our main enemy was Germany. Next day I wished him goodbye and set off on the way home with a heavy heart. From Frýdek I took the same route I had followed from Těšin - through the forest and past the farm, a way that I knew. I reached the woods about 4pm and lay down to look out for passing patrols. A few minutes later I heard someone coming. I quickly hid in the bushes, watching to see who it was.

I was very well hidden. Two men and two women were approaching but they did not see me. They were a few metres away from me, asking each other where the border was. They were surprised when I came from the bushes. I explained that the border passed through the woods where we were standing, and warned them to keep an eye on the farmhouse where the Polish patrols usually stayed. They were trying to get to Třinec, but did not know the terrain. I told them we must wait until we saw the patrol go past but after half an hour they decided they could wait no longer. It was still a long way to Třinec and they needed to arrive there before dark. I tried to persuade them to wait a bit longer but they did not want to listen and decided to go on.

I went with them – that was my big mistake. I led them from one pile of hay to the next but we were only halfway across the field when two soldiers with rifles in their hands stepped out and stopped us. They took us to their command centre in a nearby school. I told them that I did not belong to the group. The other four were taken for questioning, after which they were driven away. I do not know what happened to them. Once they had left, it was my turn to be questioned. I told them that I had gone to see a friend, not knowing that this was forbidden. They asked if I were carrying anything. I answered in the negative and it was only when they asked me to empty my pockets that I remembered I had thirty cigarettes for my father. He smoked heavily and in Těšin there were no cigarettes in the shops. Zorky, the cheapest brand I had been able to find, were sold ten at a time, wrapped in newspaper. The soldier questioning me jumped out of his chair. "You shit! You lied to me!" he yelled, hitting me so hard across the face that I fell to the floor, where he kicked me in the back, screaming like a madman. "Get up or you'll get more!"

I had tears in my eyes, and pain in my head and my back. I had to give my name, address and date of birth, but I did not know what he wrote in his report. This interrogation lasted about three hours, by which time it was already dark; because of the curfew I had to sit on the bench, cold and very hungry, until morning. I had fallen asleep when someone shook me roughly and told me I could go. It was 5am and it took me four hours to walk home. My father was furious that I had gone away and even more furious when I told him how they had treated me.

A month later we were summoned to appear before the Court. I told them that I did not know that it was forbidden to visit friends in Czechoslovakia. The judge was angrier with my father, blaming him for not keeping his family under proper control. I was given one year's probation and Father had to guarantee that he would take full responsibility that I would not break the law again. I was very sad that I had hurt him for he always worked hard to bring up his family, and I had made so much trouble for him. Instead of helping him I had caused him even more worry.

The Poles closed down the Sokol Club but we former members still met in the woods. We found a small piece of land where we played volleyball and discussed the world situation.

Chapter 3: German Occupation

On 15th March 1939 Germany occupied the rest of the Czech Lands and the next day Hitler proclaimed that Bohemia and Moravia was now a Protectorate of the Third Reich. Only Slovakia retained its autonomy by signing a treaty with Germany.

On 1st September of that year, as our family was eating dinner, a bomb exploded not far from the house. We ran outside to see what was happening, just as a second bomb flew past and exploded near the army barracks about a quarter of a mile away. My father decided immediately that my mother and sisters would be safer in the cellar. He, Ruda and I would go to the woods where we would be protected by the trees but close enough to rescue our mother and sisters if the house should be hit. Eventually the bombs stopped falling but there was a lot of noise coming from the main road which ran between Ostrava and Český Těšín. I ran to see what was happening, hoping to see our army coming back, but was shocked to see not Czech but German soldiers. Germany had invaded Poland and I remembered that Milan, my friend in Frýdek, had foreseen this. There were no Poles to be seen and German soldiers were everywhere. The Czech officer had been right when he told the Poles they would not hold Silesia for a year – after only eleven months they were running back to where they had come from.

"So, that is the end of my wages," sighed my father when I told him. During the time he had worked under the Poles he was given only a deposit on his wages and now, instead of paying the balance, they had run away. My Jewish employer believed that as a German he would be safe from persecution; he was sure that Hitler was not as bad as people thought. About a month after the German occupation he asked me to go to Brno, where his sister lived. He had not heard from her and her family for a very long time and wanted to find out if they were all right. I agreed, as I wanted to visit Leoš, from whom we had heard nothing for several months. I travelled by train to Karvina and completed the journey to Ostrava by tram. In this busy coal mining area the trams were packed with miners going to and from work and controls were less rigorous, so it was easy for me to get to Ostrava where Leoš was still working with the Criminal Police. We discussed the German occupation and I asked if he was thinking of leaving the country. He told me that he had thought about it but decided to stay as he was now married and his wife was expecting a child. He also felt that patriots would be needed inside Czechoslovakia even more than abroad.

In Brno I easily found my boss's sister, who told me they were not in danger in the Protectorate. She gave me a parcel of food for him. I was worried about getting this through the checkpoint but fortunately my brother was working there and helped me. The tram was full again, there was no check and I got safely through with my parcel. The next day I took the parcel and the letter to my employer, but found the shop was locked. On the door a notice, written in German, stated that this business was closed. When I rang the bell he opened the door and quickly pulled me inside. He was very distressed, telling me that he was not allowed to let anyone in, even to talk. He could no longer carry on business and had had to lay off all his workers, who had had to report the Employment Office, so I too must do this. He thanked me for all I had done for him. He was very sad and regretted that he had not gone to America when he had the chance. We said our goodbyes and that was the last time I saw him.

At the Employment Office I was asked why I worked for a Jew. I explained that I was learning tailoring and would like to complete my apprenticeship, but there were no vacancies in this trade and I was sent to work at a German owned dry cleaning company. As well as civilian clothes the factory cleaned a lot of German Army uniforms, many of which were very dirty and bloodstained. I was employed in the laundry where the work was very hard. It was bitterly cold in winter and in summer impossibly hot. Worst of all, I was hungry all the time. Food was rationed; the work was heavy but there was little to eat. Marie had been unable to continue her apprenticeship as Father, not having been paid his full wage for almost a year, could not afford the fee. She, too, was sent to work, pressing clothes, in the factory where I worked. Under the Germans every adult was compelled to have a job, and Emilie was allocated to a German family as a maidservant. Because of her asthma she was unfit for factory work.

I had been working there for a few months when all employees were ordered to assemble in the nearby park. There we saw many German lorries and soldiers armed with machine guns. In the middle of the park they had built a gallows about twenty five metres long, above a platform a metre high. Everyone was quiet because no one knew what this meant or why we were there. The silence was broken by the arrival of more lorries, from which twenty four men, hands bound behind their backs, were unloaded. With each man was a leather-coated guard who looked like Gestapo. An announcement in German came over the loudspeaker, but this I did not understand. Only later I learnt that these men had been sentenced to death because they had been accused of acting against the German Reich and this public execution was to serve as a warning to anyone who might have similar ideas.

The Gestapo placed the ropes round their victims' necks and the order was given to push them from the platform. One of the victims was a very tall young man about twenty years old. If he had straightened his legs he could probably have touched the ground, but he lifted them – I think he knew that nothing could help him. Finally a group of Germans went from one to the other and injected them in the chest to ensure they were dead. Many people were forced to watch this execution. Women were fainting and many were crying. I was sixteen years old and have never been able to forget the horror of what I saw that day. It was a terrifying demonstration of Nazi power, which doubled my hatred for the Germans and their oppressive regime.

It was forbidden to speak Czech. The only language permitted was German. On one occasion I remember two old people walking down the street; the woman was speaking to her husband who was deaf and didn't hear what she said. "What did you say?" he asked loudly in Czech. Walking past them was a boy, about 14 years old, wearing the Hitler Youth uniform. He stopped, yelling at them that they were in Germany and they must speak German. The old man couldn't understand him and asked what he had said. The boy hit him across the face, yelling all the time: "This is Germany. Here we speak only German." The old man's pipe fell from his mouth and it was obvious that he was bewildered and did not know what was happening. His wife, who was crying, picked up the pipe and pulled him away. People were standing round them but no one had the courage to say anything. Most people did not speak German because they did not know that language. It was a ghost town. People walked around without speaking and when they met friends they greeted them with a nod. Another unpopular ruling was that when the Hitler Youth was marching with the German flag, everyone had to stop and remove their hats and wait until they had passed.

  I was 17 years old in 1940 and was planning, with some of my Sokol friends, to escape across the border. We began spending our weekends in the mountains where a lot of young people were travelling. We sang Czech songs and wore colourful kerchiefs at our necks. The Beskydy are beautiful and we felt quite safe there. Our group of six boys had planned a way to escape along the ridge of the Beskydy into Austria and from there through the mountains to Switzerland. This would have to be in summer because we would not survive in winter conditions at that altitude. One Sunday we were again in the mountains where we had planned our escape. We had decided to leave at the end of July and this time we travelled one station further so that we were nearer to the Protectorate and could explore the mountains further ahead. At Hnojník a crowd of young men left the train and through the window we saw them surrounded by German soldiers. We quickly took off our kerchiefs in case they came to check the train and were relieved that there were no soldiers at the next station. We did not know what had happened but on the way back we heard that there had been many arrests. It was also announced that trips to the mountains were now forbidden, and any larger assemblies were banned, so our hopes to leave by this route were dashed.

At work my health suffered a lot. I had boils on my hands and neck, had lost a lot of weight and was very weak. The doctor told me that because of my health I should be doing a less arduous job. At the Employment Office my request to go back to tailoring was granted.

Early in 1941 our family was called to the Town Hall, where a Committee was deciding nationality status. My father had to prove that he was not Jewish. After a long interrogation the members of the Committee were debating and pointing to my younger brother and me. Silesia had been declared part of the Third Reich and so people living there had to have German nationality, which was divided into three categories. Group 1 was for people born in Germany, Group 2 was for Germans born in Czechoslovakia of German parents and Group 3, the Volkslist, covered the rest of the people, who were subject to further screening. Our family was classified as Group 3. Later we learned that men in Group 3 would have to join the German Army, which made my parents very unhappy. My brother and I tried to make plans to get across the border but we had no idea how hard it would be for us to escape.

I had left the dry-cleaning company and was employed by a tailor in Polish Těšin, where I had to work as an apprentice because I had not completed three years training. The wage was very small but the work was easier than in the factory and my health soon improved. I had been working there six months when I was conscripted into the German Army.

Chapter 4: With the Wehrmacht in France

In the Autumn I said goodbye to my father on the railway station where he was working. He had tears in his eyes and I too felt very upset. We did not know if we would ever see each other again. Father gave me some advice. He told me that when I was in Germany I should pretend, when spoken to or asked anything, that I did not understand the language, and then perhaps they would send me back home. On the train there were a few young men in the compartment. One started talking to me in German, but I replied in Czech that I did not understand the language, explaining that because of the long hours I had had to work during the two years of the occupation there had been no chance for me to take a course in German. He began to speak to me Czech; he had learnt German because he was employed by a German photographer. Ferda came from Bohumin. He told me that in his heart he was still Czech and suggested that we should try to stay together; he would teach me German, as otherwise I would have a very hard life. We became good friends even though it was for only a short time. When we reached our destination we had to stand in line for interrogation by a German officer. When asked my name, even though I had learnt such basics in school, I replied in Czech that I did not understand. The man began to shout, asking what kind of army it was when the troops could not speak the language. I was sent to the end of the line where a few Polish boys were standing – there were about thirty of us. The next day they shaved our heads and took us to the railway station, where we were loaded into cattle-trucks. We had no idea where they were taking us but, after many hours travel, we arrived at the town of Lillebonne in France. At the station German soldiers in riding breeches, boots and spurs were waiting for us. They belonged to a Veterinary Unit. The vets operated on horses wounded on the fighting front and when they were healthy again sent them back to the Army. Our job was to clean the horses and stables.

There were many foreigners including some black French prisoners in this unit. The office staff, the veterinarians and the soldiers guarding were all older Germans – there were no young men among them. Later we found out that their idea in sending us to this group was that we should learn their language and, after basic training, we would be ready for posting to a regular fighting unit.

Each day started with roll-call, when work was allocated. About a fortnight after my arrival they realised that I was a tailor, and I was sent to the tailors' workroom, where the Sergeant in charge was helped by two French ladies. Our job was to repair working overalls and German uniforms, especially riding-breeches. I found this work much easier, but when I was on night duty I had to do stable work. I was billeted with the Sergeant in a small room next to the workroom. Every morning I had to attend roll-call where they checked that no one was missing. We were split into two groups and taught how to ride the horses.

I belonged to the second group. One day a Polish boy from the other group had already been thrown six times and everyone, including me, was laughing at him. I did not realise that the German riding master was watching me. When I noticed this I quickly stopped laughing but it was too late. He ordered me to mount the horse. As I approached I noticed that his hand, holding the whip, was shaking. I suspected that when I tried to mount he would hit the horse and I would be sent flying, but I did not want to give him this pleasure. I remembered in Sokol using the horse in the gym. This horse was not very big so, instead of putting my leg into the stirrup as the German expected, it was easy for me to grab the saddle with both hands and pull myself up. When he swung the whip the horse kicked with his hind legs but I was already safely up and prepared for this and he did not throw me. The other horses were becoming restless during this disturbance so the trainer sent me from the ring. The horse had been wounded in the back during the fighting and when the other boy had tried to mount he must have touched the sore spot, causing the horse to buck.

Once outside, when I touched his back, he started kicking. I did this a few times and he kicked less and less, until finally he settled down. At the end of the ride he was wet with sweat and his body was covered with white foam. We were not allowed to leave a horse in this state, so in the stable I cleaned him with straw until he was dry. After grooming the horse I was sent to report to the Commanding Officer in the Chateau, where the Germans had their headquarters. I did not know what I had done wrong but thought that perhaps they had seen me when I was making the horse kick by touching his rump. However the Commanding Officer, who was also the Chief Veterinarian of this unit, told me to saddle his horse and one for myself and report back to the chateau at 1pm. It was midday and with only one hour to get everything ready I had no time for dinner. I went straight to the stables and asked a Polish comrade to help me clean and saddle the two horses. I quickly cleaned myself up and at one o'clock I was waiting for him. I heard later that all the Germans in the office were looking through the window and betting that the horse I was riding would throw me. I am happy to say they were wrong! After that I was responsible for the care of these two horses, giving me more work than before, but that was not all.

Two officers, who brought their uniforms to the workroom to be pressed and cleaned, told me I was appointed to be their batman. My job would be to clean and press their uniforms, polish their boots every morning, collect and serve breakfast, dinner and evening meal and to tidy up after the meals. This last job I did gladly because the Germans had their own kitchen and their food was a hundred times better than that given to us foreigners. For us it was water, potatoes and cabbage and sometimes, when a horse died, we got a little bit of horsemeat in our "eintopf" (food cooked in one pot). I doled out smaller portions, and if an officer asked for more I gave it to him. What was left was for me, and when there was enough I gave some to my Polish friend, Johann the blacksmith who often helped me when I was working in the stables.

One of our jobs was to take the horses to be shod. In the forge were two blacksmiths, one German and Johann, who, like me, did not speak German. When he was talking it was two words

German and ten Polish, but he was a first-class blacksmith. The first time I took a horse to the German blacksmith I had no idea what to do. The horse was big and heavy and I was very weak. I took the hind leg between my knees but because of his weight I could not hold him. The German was yelling at me but I did not understand what I was doing wrong. When he was nailing the shoe the horse suddenly kicked out and I finished on the fence. Johann quickly came to calm the horse and afterwards showed me the right way to hold him. The German was hurt so Johann had to finish the job; he explained that I should not let the horse lean on me and told me that in future it would be better to let him shoe my horses.

One morning, after finishing my work for my two officers, I was late for the 7am roll-call. The Sergeant-in-charge spotted me trying to join the line. He called me out and ordered me to run round the parade ground, alternately lying down and standing up on his order, always when I was near a puddle. There were plenty of these as it had been raining heavily. When, wet and covered in mud, I went to rejoin the line, he yelled that I was filthy and gave me five minutes to clean myself up. I washed my face and swilled my overalls in water to get rid of the mud. Wet through, I ran back to the roll-call, which was already finishing, so I was late again. The Sergeant started yelling at me again and gave me a punishment called "Kraft durch Freude" ("Strength through Joy") which meant tidying the muckheap from 6pm to 9pm.

When I came back to the workroom still in my wet overalls the tailor, who had seen what had happened, was very angry. I could not work in wet clothes so he found me some dry overalls, sent to us for repair. I did not know how I would be able to serve my officers their evening meal and prepare their uniforms for the morning, as well as do my punishment. Telling me that he would sort things out he left the workroom. On his return he told me I should do my usual work for the officers The punishment had been cancelled and in future I need not attend morning roll-call, but he warned me not to walk past the parade-ground at that time.

The other Sergeant became my biggest enemy. Once, on stable duty, I was carrying a bale of hay on my back but, as I tried to bend to get through the door, my knee gave way and I could not get up again. This Sergeant was passing and kicked the bale of hay from me. Swearing at me, he hit me across the back with the bridle and bit he was carrying. One of the Poles working outside came to help me with the bale. My back was very painful for a long time and after that I always tried to avoid him as much as I could.

German officers often brought their uniforms to us for repair or pressing. On one occasion two of them showed their true character. One of our French helpers was a lady of about fifty, whom we called "Madame." The other, Denise, was about twenty-five; she was not particularly nice looking, but she wore lots of heavy makeup and thought she was beautiful. She was always flirting with the Germans, who usually ignored or made fun of her. On this particular day the two officers were talking together and Denise was fussing round them, touching them, laughing all the time and behaving like a little girl. At first they took no notice of her but she kept pushing herself between them. She sat on the pressing table, pulling up her skirt, and instead of sewing, she opened her handbag, took out lipstick and mirror and started to make up her face. I could not understand what the officers said to each other, but they suddenly grabbed her, put her on the table and pulled down her knickers. The stupid girl was still laughing. One took her lipstick and painted between her legs. The second took a toothbrush from her handbag; when he started to use this between her legs it must have hurt a lot because she began to scream. I was sitting by the sewing-machine but neither the tailor nor I dared help her. To begin with, Madame did not say anything but when Denise started to scream she jumped from her chair and went between them to protect the girl. She was yelling and cursing – I didn't understand a lot of the words but she called them pigs and threatened to report them to the Commanding

Officer. At first they laughed but soon they quietened down and left. The Sergeant tried to calm the women but they took their coats and went away. The next day they did not come to work.

Later the two officers came in and it was obvious that they were worried about what could develop from this. They had a long discussion with the Sergeant, who told me that if anyone should ask me I had seen nothing. This was partly true, as I had been sitting at the sewing-machine with my back to the room. In the end no one asked me anything about this episode – perhaps they managed to sort it out between themselves or maybe the women did not report it. They never returned to work, so now the Sergeant and I had even more to do.

One hour each day was set aside for training us foreign workers. One day this would be German language, the next day we would have basic training in marching and the use of firearms. Because I had extra duties (looking after two horses for the Commanding Officer and acting as batman for the two officers) I was excused the marching exercises, but like everyone else I had to attend the German classes and the firearms training.

At the firing range we were once given three bullets each. I remembered how when I was young the forester had taught us to shoot. He always pushed the rifle firmly into his armpit before lining up the sight, held his breath and slowly squeezed the trigger. On our target the rings were numbered from one to twelve from the outside of the circle. With my first shot I hit ten on the right; at my second attempt I hit eleven to the left, which showed that I had over-corrected. The third bullet hit the twelve straight in the centre. The German supervisor could not believe his eyes and asked an officer to look at the target. As they talked I heard words like "school," and "sharpshooter". I realised with shock and fright that my stupid showing-off had demonstrated that I knew how to use a gun and they would probably transfer me to a fighting unit, where I did not want to go. If I were to fight I wanted it to be for my own country, not for Nazi Germany. The officer gave me another three bullets. This time I did not try. My first attempt hit eight on the right, my second seven left and the third was six at the top. He just waved his hand and said that my first round had been sheer luck. We went to the range twice more, but I always made sure that I did not shoot well.

In August 1942 there was an alarm, with heavy traffic on the roads. Patrols and guards were everywhere and we were ordered to pack all our equipment into wagons, ready for immediate departure. The horses were already hitched and those of us who were not allocated to a wagon were each given a saddled horse and a further three horses to lead. In case the chateau had to be evacuated in a hurry, we had to be ready to travel at a moment's notice. We heard that the English were landing in Dieppe.

I was very happy, thinking that I now had a chance to get away from the Germans I hated so much. The chateau had a large garden and a small wood, where we were ordered to stay through the night. In the morning I was quite disappointed because I had expected that by then the English would have arrived. We returned to our quarters but remained in a state of readiness. The news that only a small group of troops had landed and that the Germans had taken them all prisoner was very disheartening.

Within a few days everything was back to normal. The Germans were bragging that their army was so strong and that they had pushed the English back into the sea. I took this very badly. I was worried that they would send me to a fighting unit – and I did not want to fight on the German side. A few of the other foreigners who had come with me had already left. I think I was still there firstly because I was needed in the tailoring workroom, where we were now only two since the women had left, and secondly because I was batman to the two German officers.

I had one very unpleasant experience, which terrified me. Because I had so much work I got up very early in the morning to get through everything. When I finished about 9pm I was very tired and soon fell asleep. One evening the German officer, who was in charge of the Proviant (food distribution), came to visit the Sergeant tailor. They were talking and drinking late into the night. In the end the officer said that as it was too late for him to get back to his quarters he would sleep with the Sergeant but was told that, because the bed was too small for two, he would have to share mine. I was half asleep when the German climbed into my bed. I turned my back but suddenly felt his hand touching me between my legs and playing with my penis. It was a terrifying feeling. I realised what he was doing. I jumped out of bed, saying I was going to the lavatory and ran into the workroom next to the bedroom. After locking the door I lay down on the pressing table and covered myself with some coats, which were there for repair.

A few minutes later he came to look for me. He tried the door and when he found it was locked he knew where I was. He started telling me I must not be afraid, that he would not do anything to me and it was only human for two men to like each other. I was very quiet. I did not answer him and felt the gooseflesh on my back. After a while he changed his tone and harshly ordered me to open the door or he would smash it down. I was terrified, shaking, and looking round for something with which to protect myself. I grabbed the large tailoring shears and waited to see what would happen. He started shaking the door, making a lot of noise, when I heard a voice in the passage, wanting to know who was making the racket. It was a German shoemaker whose room and workroom was next to ours. He came from the area near the Polish border and spoke some Polish. The officer trying to break into my hiding-place left after this interruption. I stayed there until morning because I was afraid that he might come back.

The next day the shoemaker asked me what the noise had been about. I told him everything and said that I was afraid that he would come after me again. He assured me that I did not need to worry – homosexuality was forbidden and if it came out the officer could face a court martial. He also told me that he would warn this man that he would report him if he ever again tried anything like this. I was very grateful to him and it never happened again. This misadventure frightened me very much. I was a very naïve young boy and had no idea that such a relationship existed between men.

By the end of 1942 all the black prisoners from the French Army, who had been working in the stables alongside us from Eastern Europe, had been taken away.

Chapter 5: Move to Russia

At the beginning of 1943 we were preparing to leave. We had no idea where we were going when, at the end of February, we were loaded on to a train. We took only the healthy horses and about ten fully loaded wagons, each pulled by four horses. I was allocated to ride the two leading horses on the blacksmith's wagon. We also had two large transport lorries, normally used to collect wounded horses. The rest of the sick horses were taken away. We travelled through Germany, Czechoslovakia and Poland but our final destination was Russia. When we disembarked somewhere near Kiev we were told that our job would be collecting the wounded horses left behind by the fighting troops. It was spring, the snow was thawing and the roads were impassable. Several times we had to stop to help when wagons carrying supplies to the front had become bogged down in the mud.

Our unit was always billeted at collective farms where stables and food for the horses were available. We were put up in the farm-labourers' houses which were very poor, usually consisting of just one room with a sanded earth floor. In one half of the room was the large stove used for cooking, and on top of which the family slept; in the other half stood a large table with benches round it. These benches were also used for sleeping. Two of us were put in each house. We were given some straw on the floor in the corner and that is where we slept. There was no electricity. A piece of string soaked in a small tin of oil burned all the time and when they needed to make a fire they lit it from this little flame. There were no lavatories and to relieve themselves they went behind the barn, or, in winter, in the corner of the barn there was a plank of wood over a hole in the ground. In the dark one had to be very careful not to fall into this hole. Early one morning I had gone outside to relieve myself. As I was squatting there a woman ran suddenly from the house. She must have had diarrhoea. She did not see me, lifted her skirt, and nearly covered me. I coughed to warn her that she was not alone; she dropped her skirt and ran away.

These were kind-hearted people. Though they did not have enough for themselves they always gave us a little of their food, even if it was only a few potatoes. Matches were difficult to find and for one little box I got ten eggs. Most of them could not read or write and in these small villages there were no schools or shops. For their work on the collectives they were paid in kind. Money had no value for them because there was nothing to buy. To travel to a bigger town could take them one or two days.

The Ukrainian language has a lot of similarities to Czech and very soon I managed to make myself understood. They were very keen to find out what was happening in the world and in our own countries. They liked to hear how we lived, about cinemas, dancing, etc. When I told them that I went to school for eight years they thought I was a professor. I felt very sorry for them; they were poor, frightened, and very superstitious. For example, if the little flame, which burned day and night in each house, went out they were sure that someone in the house would die. Whistling in the house was forbidden – they believed this was calling the devil. They still observed many old customs. In one village, where we arrived late at night, they were celebrating the birth of a child in the house where I was billeted. As soon as I walked in I was offered a glass of home-made alcohol. They were holding pieces of green fern, which they dipped into the drink, sprinkled my face and gave me a kiss on the cheek. After that I had to drink to the health of the child. It was one of their customs, and not to offend them I knocked back the drink which was definitely not good for my health.

Next day when we resumed our journey I was very ill. Drinking the alcohol on an empty stomach was not a good thing to do. I was sick during the night, and in the morning felt so faint that I could scarcely stand. We had another day's travelling in front of us and I did not know how I would get into the saddle. I was so weak that after a few attempts I was still trying to mount. I begged one of the Polish boys, who was sitting next to the driver on the wagon, to change places with me but forgot to tell him that both these horses had been wounded in the fighting and could not bear anything to touch their hind legs. They were very good horses and I understood them. Going uphill everything was fine but when we started to go downhill my Polish comrade did not realise that he had to take care that the wooden crossbar did not catch the backs of their legs. When it did they just went mad and bolted. He was not prepared for this and fell off his horse. Both horses were galloping so fast that the wagon driver could not hold them. These were similar to the covered wagons of the American West and I clung to one of the hoops so that I would not fall off.

When the Germans realised what was happening they galloped ahead, to catch the leading horses and stopped them. They were very angry when they saw that I had not been riding. I tried to explain that I was sick, but they ordered me to get into the saddle. When I was climbing down from the wagon my legs gave way and I fell. Though I dragged myself up and tried to put my foot into the stirrup I was so weak that I could not lift my leg. In the end they realised how ill I was, called for another rider and put me into the back of the wagon. As I lay between the cases and the wagon was bouncing along the rough road I thought my last day had come. It was a great relief when we finally stopped. Johann, the blacksmith, took care of me. He gave me herbal tea to drink, which eventually helped. I think I had alcohol poisoning.

The names of the villages and collective farms I cannot remember – it is possible that some were identified only by a number. Usually the collective would be built first and then a few houses for the workers. I remember that we stayed longer than usual at one farm, near the town of Berdičev. The stables and buildings were bigger than those we had stayed in previously. Again I was given the job of looking after the two officers whom I had been serving in France. We were billeted in the house of the headman of the village, whose wife still lived there. Her husband had had to leave with the Russian Army when they were retreating.

The house had three rooms. The officers occupied the bedroom. The second room had a table and benches, with a mattress on the floor in the corner, where I slept. Our hostess, who was about forty, slept in the kitchen. This was a very big farm. There were two large stables and a barn full of hay and oats for the horses, which suited the Germans very well. There was also a smaller building, used as a school, where the other foreign labourers were billeted. The Germans occupied the rooms in the large building, where they also had an office.

Our job was to collect wounded horses, left behind in the villages as the army advanced further into Russia, but we soon discovered there were no such horses. It looked like the villagers had used them for meat. When the Germans realised this they started collecting healthy Russian horses. We soon had quite a lot of these, which were guarded by about thirty Russian prisoners, who slept in the stables. I had plenty of work, looking after my two officers and their horses.

On our second night I was lying on my mattress, half asleep, when the door opened and someone approached my corner very quietly. I thought someone was breaking into the house and was ready to jump out when I realised it was the lady of the house, carrying a little candle in her hand. I pretended to be asleep; after waiting a few seconds, she went to join the officer in the bedroom. I could hear them making love but wondered how they could understand each other – the German did not speak Russian and she did not understand German. The next day, when she asked, I told her I had slept very well, but I could see she had something on her mind.

Once, when the Germans were having a party in their offices, they sent me to invite the teacher to join them. She was young and attractive, perhaps about thirty years old, and slept in a small room next to the school. I explained why I had come but she declined the invitation, saying that she was not well. She asked where I came from and why I was with the Germans. We talked for about quarter of an hour when she suddenly stroked my face and invited me inside. I had to tell the Germans why she could not come to their party, but she wanted me to come back later as she had a lot of questions to ask. As soon as I had delivered her message I returned to her house. The room where she was living was very small – a bed and table were the only furniture. We sat on the bed and she asked my age, saying that I looked very young. I told her I was twenty. Then she wanted to know if I had a girl at home. I explained that my homeland had been occupied first by the Poles and then by the Germans, and because I had to work very late nights there had been no time for girls. "Poor thing! You are missing the best years of your life", she whispered, putting her arms round my shoulders. I held her in my arms and what followed was the most wonderful thing that had ever happened to me. That evening I lost my virginity in the nicest possible way. She was very gentle and we made love a few times. I never realised that anything so beautiful existed. She invited me to call again the next evening, but warned me not to come through the door – she would leave the window open for me. She did not want anyone to see us together. After that I visited her whenever I could.

    About a fortnight later we were preparing to move again. Winter had started and it was snowing heavily. Day after day the Germans were experiencing major problems. The small Russian ponies could easily run on top of the snow but the heavy German horses kept falling through, bogging down their transport columns. I acted as interpreter when the Germans were looking for food for the horses, which was difficult to find in the winter. They had decided that mules would be more suitable, and would solve their transport problems, so one day an older German soldier and I were sent to a railway station, where the mules were expected. Our job was to guide the column to our collective, which was about four hours' ride from the station. When we reached the railway there was no sign of the train. We waited a couple of days until one of the railwaymen told us that it was unlikely it would arrive. There was so much snow on the line that rail traffic could not get through. We decided we had better return to our unit and explain the situation. The front was not very far away and we could hear the sound of the artillery.

When we finally got back to the village our unit was no longer there. They had left a message for us to follow them to the next village, the name of which I can no longer remember. They had been ordered to move because the front was coming nearer. When I asked the villagers for directions they just pointed out the direction we should take.

The Ukraine is a vast, open country, especially when covered in snow. We could not see the road; there were no telegraph poles or trees to act as markers. Because I knew that our unit would eventually need trains to move on, I asked where the railway ran. As it was nearly dark we decided to leave early next morning. The villages are quite a distance apart and sometimes it can take a day to make the journey, especially in winter with snow up to two metres deep. I wondered what would have happened if the train with the mules had arrived. What could we have done with them? We reached the next village that evening but our unit had stayed there only one night. We were two days behind them.

Next day we rode on again and it was already dark when we found another village. I was shocked to hear our unit had never been there. When I asked the way to the railway they pointed back the way we had come. It looked like we had been given wrong information at our last stop or we had started walking in circles. As a precaution I asked a few other people and when they all said the same thing I was satisfied that these directions were correct. There was no collective here, so we had to find somewhere to stable our horses for the night. In the end we found a small barn with hay and straw.

Two women, two old men and three children were living in the house attached to the barn. This was very small with only one room, containing a huge stove, a table and some benches. They slept on top of the stove and on the benches. There was no room for us in the house but they said we could sleep in the barn with the horses. They gave us some soup called borscht, which warmed us up a bit. We stayed in the room with them until nearly midnight. It was warm there and we did not look forward to moving to the cold barn. The old German with me could not speak a word of Russian, so he just sat by the table and because he was tired he was nodding off. One of the women said they too were tired, so we should call it a day and all go to bed. It was freezing outside and bitterly cold in the barn. We needed our sheepskin coats to keep warm, but realised we had left them in the house. I went to collect them but when I got to the door I heard the Russians talking inside. I listened for a few minutes and what I heard made my blood run cold. They were discussing how to overpower us. They decided to do this in the morning when we would be sleeping. I waited in the cold for a few minutes before banging on the door, and explained that we had forgotten our coats. When I returned to the barn I did not tell my companion what I had heard because I did not know how he would react. He wrapped himself in his coat and was soon snoring, but I could not sleep. I saddled the horses and watched that no one was coming to get us while we slept. Before we went to Russia I was always thinking of how I could escape from the Germans and hide until I could give myself up to the Allies but an incident on one of the collective farms made me think again.

Four Poles escaped from our unit and tried to join the partisans. Other Poles had refused to go with them. Later the Germans found the four men in the woods, shot and without their clothes. It looked like the partisans didn't believe that they were not pro-German and had killed them. This incident taught me that I could trust nobody.

About 4am I roused my companion, telling him that we had a long journey ahead of us and we must leave. He did not want to go – he was tired. I told him he could stay if he wished, but I was going. I also told him that the Russians were not far away and they would look after him. He woke up very fast. As we plodded through the snow I looked back all the time to check that our footprints were in a straight line. I was worried that we would start walking round in circles We were both very tired – it was hard going, as we had to travel on foot to lead the horses because they kept falling through the snow and I had not slept the night before. I did not want to sit down to rest; I had the feeling that if I did I would not get up again. My German companion was in a very bad state. He constantly moaned that he could not see, he would not live through it and he would never see his wife and children again. He showed me a very nice picture of his wife, son and daughter. I told him that he should keep looking at it and must not forget that his children were waiting for him. I was giving him advice, when I myself needed some guidance on how to get through this ordeal.

At last, after plodding along all day, we reached a village through which our unit had passed three days before. They were heading for a railway-station where there was supposed to be a very big collective farm. We were very hungry and completely exhausted – my sleepless night was affecting me. We were allowed to spend the night in one of the houses, where we slept so heavily that we did not wake up until dinner time the next day. I was afraid to set out on the next stage of our journey – it usually took a whole day to progress from one village to the next. Every time we stopped I asked where the road was, where the railway ran and where we could find a large collective – that was our only chance of finding our unit. I asked if there was a road nearby, where lorries or cars were travelling. Finally I learned that the motor road ran next to the railway. Our unit had some very heavy wagons, which needed four horses to pull them, and they would need to go on such a road.

After a good rest we left early the next day. A few hours later we found a road showing signs of recent use It looked like vehicles with chains or tracks had used it. The snow was very firm so we were able to mount our horses again but after about half an hour my horse started slipping. I discovered that in some parts there was ice under the snow. My legs were stiff from sitting in the saddle so I decided to go on foot; the road was quite firm and I could walk more quickly. My companion, who was only semi-conscious, stayed on his horse. I talked to him all the time and was watching that he did not fall off. If he hurt himself I knew I would not be able to lift him and if I had to leave him on the road he would freeze to death.

After walking for a few hours I saw in the distance some large buildings and we eventually found our unit there. Everybody was surprised that we had managed to find them. It was ten days since we had left them to go to the railway station for the mules and nobody knew where we were. They took my German companion from his horse. He was too stiff with cold to move and was unable to stand. The next day they took him away, probably to hospital. I was so tired that I went into the corner of the stable and lay on some straw where I fell asleep immediately. I had not slept long when someone kicked me in the back, yelling that I had not reported my whereabouts. I stood up but at first I did not know where I was. There were several Germans standing around me; the Commanding Officer of the unit was there, along with the two officers to whom I acted as batman and the Sergeant in charge of the stables, who was the worst German I ever met. He was probably in his civilian life a farm-worker, who worked with horses, and now he had rank he liked to throw his weight about. He did not dare yell at the Germans so he treated us foreigners like cattle. My legs were starting to buckle so I leant against the wall so as not to fall down. The Sergeant started yelling again, ordering me to stand to attention and give a report. I tried, but when I moved away from the wall my legs gave way under me and I fell to the ground. I was trying to get up and saw that the Sergeant was going to kick me again. The Commandant also noticed and shouted at him, asking him what he thought he was doing. Everything happened in a few seconds – my two officers quickly came and helped me to my feet and took me to the house, where they put me on a bench. They started to question me, but I was only half conscious and could not take everything in. I was probably saying I was hungry, but I cannot remember. They gave me some soup, which bucked me up a bit. I was vaguely aware of my whereabouts but I was completely exhausted.

When I was on the road I had told myself all the time that I must carry on; I was taking one step at a time, even though I hardly knew I was walking. Now I had the feeling that I had no need to walk another step and the relief was so great that I just wanted to fall asleep, and it did not matter where. When they realised I was only semi-conscious they gave me a blanket and I lay down on the bench. They were trying to pull off my boots, which I had not taken off the whole ten days we had been away. I had been afraid that, if I did, I would not be able to get them on again. My left leg was very painful and when they tried to take the boot off the pain made me nearly jump out of my skin. They called the first-aider but he could do nothing until the boots were off. The only thing they could do was to cut them off. They saw that my leg was infected – the skin was white and partly septic. After they had put a dressing on it I immediately fell asleep.

Chapter 6: Sick Leave

The next few days I did nothing. I could not wear my riding boots so I was sent to work in the tailoring workroom where I did not need them. Because there was no medication available to treat my leg, the infection got worse. I was called to the office to be told that I was to be transferred from the labour unit to the army. I pointed out that, because my leg was not yet healed, I was unable to wear riding boots. After conferring among themselves, they told me I could take two weeks' leave. After my leave I was to report to the Army Headquarters in Kiev and they would decide to which unit I should go. I was happy that I could go home to Těšin and was hoping that perhaps after this fortnight at home the Red Army would have pushed the Germans out of Russia and I would not have to go back there. I had no idea how difficult it would be to get out of Russia.

Firstly I could not get my boots on. Eventually I found a pair a few sizes too big, which I padded out with rags and put extra bandages on the leg so that the leather would not rub my skin. I found it very difficult to walk in them but I did not care. The important thing was that I was going home.

The next problem was how to get to the railway station, which was about three hours' walk away. With these overlarge boots I would never make it on foot. I managed to get to the road, about three hundred metres from the farm, and waited there, hoping I could get a lift from some passing vehicle. In three hours, only two lorries had passed and they would not stop, even though I waved to them. I was afraid I would never get away. When I was leaving the unit my two officers had given me a bottle of cognac and wished me luck in the future. When I remembered this I decided that if someone came along I would wave the bottle. This did the trick. An hour later a passing halftrack stopped. There were two soldiers in the cab but the back was empty. They accepted my offer of the bottle of cognac in exchange for a lift to the railway. There was no room in the front, but I did not mind sitting in the back. The only thing that mattered was that I could get to the station. The going was very slow and the journey took two hours. I was half frozen but the thought that I was going home kept me warm. When eventually we reached the station a train was ready to depart. I had no idea where it was going – all I cared about that I was getting out of this Hell. It was full of soldiers and there were still a lot of men outside trying to board. I was limping quite badly because the big boots were rubbing my wound, and I was in a lot of pain. As I was hobbling past one of the wagons someone called through a half opened window that they had room for one more. When I got on the step I realised that I would not be able to get into the wagon because it was packed, but looking round, I saw in a corner there was a little door slightly open and somebody called me to go there. It was a toilet and there were already four soldiers inside. When they noticed my limp they thought I was wounded and they made a place for me. I was sitting on the loo and they were standing around me. There was no other space. I was very lucky that I managed to get on that train. Many soldiers who could not get inside were standing on the steps. It was already going dark and starting to freeze and when the train set off some of them could not hold on and fell off.

Everyone had to leave the train in Lvov. We were taken to a large building, which I think was the army barracks. We were each given a basket in which to place all our clothes, together with a ticket bearing our name; then we were given carbolic soap and sent to the showers. I was afraid that, if they got wet, my bandages would need changing; if anyone saw how bad my leg was they would probably send me to hospital instead allowing me to go home. Instead of the shower I went to the washbasin and washed my head and body where there was hair. In the next room we were sprayed with some kind of powder against lice. The baskets with our clothes were fumigated at very high temperature to kill any fleas. When I came to dress myself I was shocked to find my riding-breeches had shrunk. I had only this one pair and wondered how I was going to get home without breeches. Fortunately, when I looked closely I realised that only the leather had shrunk so I used a knife to take it off. Now I could get into the breeches, but the seams, which had been covered by the leather, were outside instead of inside. (In riding-breeches the seams cannot be inside, as they would rub one's legs and cause blistering.) Luckily my overcoat covered the raw edges, so they were not noticeable.

It took me three days to get home. Before I left my unit I had been told that immediately I arrived in Těšin I must go to the local hospital where they would attend to my leg. I was also given an envelope to give to the German command in Kiev when I returned to Russia. The next day I went to the hospital, where they replaced my bandages and told me not to wear the riding boots because the leather rubbing against the infected part would prevent it healing quickly. I had to go every other day to have the dressing changed. Five days later I decided to visit Leoš in Ostrava, where he was still working for the criminal police. He had married soon after my last visit in 1939; at his flat his wife and little boy greeted me and in the evening I met my brother again after four years. I told him of my experiences in France and Russia.

About nine-o'clock the next morning I was awakened by someone banging on the door. Outside were two men, checking a report that there were more people in the flat than were registered. The flat had a bedroom, living room, kitchen and bathroom. My brother, his wife and child occupied the bedroom and I was sleeping on the settee in the living room. Both men were very rude; they came into the living room and when they saw me they wanted to know my name and what I was doing there. I told them that I was visiting my brother. My brother's surname was Valica, so they immediately wanted to check my identity papers because of the difference in our surnames. As I got up from the settee and pulled off the blanket they saw that my leg was bandaged and asked how I had been wounded. I handed over my papers, together with the official letter to the hospital, date-stamped each time I went for treatment. Everything was written in German and my papers bore the official stamp, confirming that I belonged to the Veterinary Unit. I also told them that my brother was my stepbrother, from my mother's first marriage. They looked at each other and in a more friendly tone asked why I had not reported to the police that I was living in the flat. I informed them that when I had arrived late the previous evening it was too late to report, and that my brother, who was working at the police station, would register me that morning. They made notes of this and left.

When Leoš came home at dinnertime we told him what had happened. His wife was still shaking – she thought they had come to arrest me. Leoš knew I had to register but, because of my late arrival, he thought this morning would be soon enough. He also told me that he was sure someone from one of the six families living in this block of flats was an informer. He felt that he could no longer trust anyone.

I decided I would go back home so that I would not cause them any more trouble – and I was due to go to the hospital the next day to have my bandages changed. Leoš asked me to wait until 4pm, when he would finish work, so that he could go with me to the tram station. I said goodbye to his wife and son and we left together. He wanted to talk to me but not in front of Hilda, who was very nervous and living all the time in fear. He asked if I had considered going over to join one of the Czech units fighting with the Russians. I had thought about this quite a lot while I was in Russia and would have liked to join the Czech army. The problem was the very severe winter and to find somewhere to hide was difficult as the local people could not be trusted. I told him about the Poles who ran away from the Germans and were found murdered in the woods and also of my experience when we were trying to rejoin our unit and I overheard our hosts planning to overpower us as we slept. I emphasised that one could not trust Russians. I asked if there was any chance I could hide in this area so that I need not go back to Russia. He told me that it would be impossible; I would not survive in the mountains in winter and to hide with a family was too dangerous as everywhere there were German spies, who reported any stranger to the authorities. I had seen what happened in their flat that morning.

We were walking past the park as we talked. The street was empty except for one man with a dog walking towards us. As he passed my brother barely whispered the greeting "Nazdar." The man did not answer but as he pulled out a handkerchief to wipe his nose a key fell from his pocket. Leoš picked it up and called out to him. He walked towards him and, as he handed over the key, they exchanged a few words before the man walked away. Leoš told me that he had done a very silly thing. He explained that he knew this man from Sokol and that they still used among themselves the forbidden greeting "Nazdar", but not in public, only when they were alone. Even though he had explained that I was his brother his friend had insisted that not even one's own family could be trusted. When I asked what this meant he said that he could not tell me more and it was better that we did not discuss it. After the war, when I asked him again about this conversation, he admitted a few members of Sokol were helping the Underground. Those in the police force, if they saw any names on the list of those suspected by the Germans, would pass this information on to them. (The man in the street was one of the couriers passing on such information.)

We said goodbye at the station. The tram was packed so I had to stand until a few people got off and I found a seat. When a German soldier boarded at the next stop the tram conductor, a young man in his twenties, was looking for a place for him. "Hey, you! Get up!" he called out when he saw me. "I need your seat." Much to his annoyance, I took no notice. "Are you deaf, idiot?" he roared. "Get up". (I must explain that because of my wound I was unable to wear my riding boots, so was wearing civilian clothes). A lady in front of me, probably to help the situation, stood up, saying that the soldier could have her seat as she was getting off at the next stop. The conductor, obviously displeased, brought a uniformed policeman from the front of the tram. I do not know what the conductor had said but the policeman asked in German for my papers. These I gave to him, along with the letter to the hospital, where it was written that I had to go for regular treatment. The papers were stamped by the Veterinary Unit and everything was written in German. The policeman read this and gave it back to me. "Alles in Ordnung. Kranke Soldat" ("All in order. Wounded soldier") he told the conductor, who did not know where to look or what to do. When I was getting off at the last stop I saw the conductor chatting to the policeman, which meant that he understood German.

On my last day at home, when I went to the hospital for treatment I asked the doctor if he could extend my leave until my leg was healed. I explained that I would find it very difficult to wear the riding boots. Unfortunately, as a civilian doctor in a civilian hospital, he could do nothing, but suggested I should report to the army hospital. The nurse put a little more wadding round my leg so the boots would not press on the wound too much. This caused another slight problem – the extra padding made it impossible to put on my trousers, which were very narrow from the knee down. To get them on I had to open the seam on the left leg and now had to figure out a way to get the unpicked leg into my boots. Eventually I put another bandage outside the breeches and this filled the space in my oversized boots.

My leave was over and I had to go back to Russia, where I did not wish to be. In the train I stood by the window and looked towards my beloved Beskydy Mountains, thinking I would never see them again. My orders were to present the letter from the Veterinary Group to the German Headquarters in Kiev; there I would be given my new posting to a fighting unit. I held this letter in my hand, wondering what would happen if I lost it. The more I thought about it the more the idea appealed to me. I was hoping to be sent back to my former group in the Veterinary Corps. This would give me extra time to point out that my leg was not properly healed. I let the letter blow away through the window and, when I finally reached Kiev, handed over only my identity documents.

Chapter 7: Back to France

When the German clerk checked his list he told me that my unit was no longer in Russia. I felt sick with disappointment, but his superior officer curtly ordered him to give me travel documents to France. My heart was beating fast and my hand was shaking as I took my new papers. I left quickly and hurried to the railway station before they could change their minds. I completely forgot how hard it was to walk in my large boots – the only thing on my mind was how quickly I could get away. I climbed on to a train, which was ready to leave – I did not even know where it was going. Once aboard I learnt that it was bound for Warsaw. When we reached our destination I was heartened to see a field-kitchen serving soup. After eating my soup I caught a train to Berlin, took a seat in the corner and soon fell asleep. Then Army Control shook me awake, demanding my travel documents. After checking my papers, I was told that my documents were not valid for this express train. They again examined my papers, which still contained the letter from the hospital. When I told them I was coming from Russia they looked at each other and then the man in charge told me not to get on an express train next time. Looking round I realised all the other passengers were officers. When I had boarded there had been no one in the compartment; it had filled up while I slept. The Germans had great sympathy for anyone coming from the Russian front where they had suffered heavy losses. I must have looked very poor in my big boots and shabby overcoat. The officers ignored me and no one sat next to me, for which I was grateful. I was soon asleep again. In Berlin I ate more soup and this time I was careful to catch a normal train to Paris. This was full of soldiers returning from leave. The journey was long as the train made many stops, but this was a good thing because on every station soup was available.

When we reached Paris I was ordered to rejoin my unit, now stationed in Mauzé. I left the train in Bordeaux, where I recognized an officer who confirmed that he too was going back to the Veterinary Unit, so I travelled with him. When I reported to the Unit Office they were very surprised to see me and wanted to know what I was doing there. I showed them my travel documents and told them (untruthfully, I am afraid) that I had handed in my letter at Kiev as instructed. I was told I could stay with the unit for the time being and I was given my old job in the tailoring workroom.

A week later I was called to the office and informed that the authorities in Russia were looking for me and that I would be sent back there. To me this was a bitter blow. Because my leg had not completely healed I decided that I must do something to avoid being sent to the Eastern Front. I removed the bandage, scratched the scab from my wound, and covered it with dust from sweeping the workroom. I did this several times over the next few days and the infection flared up again. When my orders for Russia came through I told them, quite truthfully, that my leg was still painful and I could not walk in the boots. The two officers, for whom I acted as batman, spoke to the Commanding Officer, who sent me to hospital for a check-up; this medical report would decide my future.

I bandaged my leg myself without any medication so the wound did not look very good. At the hospital the nurse took me to a room, told me to strip naked and lie on the table until the doctor came. It was not long before he came in, along with a nurse who stood behind my head. She was young and very beautiful and there was I, without a stitch of clothing. I quickly put my hand over my private parts, which were showing signs of arousal and I began to sweat. The other nurse, who was a little older noticed my embarrassment and quickly covered me with a white towel. Instead of letting the nurses carefully remove the bandage the doctor cut through it and ripped it off. The gauze was sticking to my skin and this opened the wound so that pus and blood started pouring out. When he saw the state of my leg he told the older nurse to clean it up and re-bandage it. He then wrote something on the form I had brought with me, and he left with the younger nurse, for which I was thankful – her presence excited me too much and I was ashamed that I did not manage to control myself. On my return to the office they told me that I was unfit for service in Russia. In Mauzé I was doing the same work as before. I was batman to the two officers and responsible for the care of two horses. The rest of the time I worked in the tailoring workshop.

The Veterinary Unit was stationed in a large chateau with extensive stables in the centre of the town. The entry from the main street was guarded by a large gatehouse. Here the guards used the ground floor, and in the top two rooms were the tailoring workshop and the bedroom for the German tailor and myself. The sewing-machine was by the window where the light was better. Most of my time was spent sewing on the machine and several times I noticed that in a house across the road someone was watching us. Every time I looked up this person would step quickly away from the window. I mentioned this to Johann, my blacksmith friend. He was always very keen on the girls and told me that a blonde French girl lived there; she always smiled at him when he walked past.

One Sunday, when we walked past, the blonde was sitting on a bench in the garden. "Kochana děvčina", (which means "Beautiful girl."), Johann greeted her in Polish. We walked around the town for a while and when we came back the girl was still there. She came to the gate and spoke to us in French, which I did not understand. The only word I caught was "café" – my knowledge of the language was limited to "please" and "thank you." Johann knew a little more than I did, and spoke a mixture of French, German and Polish; he told me she was asking us to join her for a cup of coffee. I did not believe him until she opened the gate and beckoned us inside. Johann did not hesitate and I went too.

Inside she invited us to sit by the table and she went into the kitchen to make the coffee. While we were waiting I asked Johann in Polish how we would talk to her as neither of us understood French, but he told me not to worry; we would manage somehow. Suddenly the door opened and a man about thirty years old came in and began speaking to us in Polish. We did not want to believe what we heard. We were looking at him like idiots. He had heard us talking Polish and wanted to know who we were. We explained that we were from Silesia, which was now occupied by Germany and people who lived in that area had to serve in the German army. He wanted to know what type of unit we were in and what the Russians were doing there. He had heard them singing. We told him that we were with a Veterinary Unit and the Russians were prisoners working in the stables. When we asked him what he was doing there he explained that he worked in France but was visiting in Mauzé. He asked us not to tell anyone we had seen him. He also mentioned that he had heard that in England there were Polish and Czech army units. After that meeting we never saw him again.

I was still responsible for cleaning and exercising two horses. My usual route was along a lane through the fields – about two kilometres there and back. On one of my daily rides I noticed a farm and went there to try to buy some eggs; I still had a few marks my parents had given me when I was leaving home. In the farmyard I asked the farmer, in my poor French, if he had any eggs for sale. "Marie, máš tam vejce? ("Marie, have you any eggs?") he called to someone in the house. I was really surprised to hear him speaking my language. When I asked in Czech, where he came from he told me that he was Slovak and invited me inside. I tied my horses to the fence and went in gladly. He offered me food and asked what I was doing in France. After talking to him for about an hour I had to go, or the Germans would want to know where I had been for so long. He gave me twenty eggs but when I wanted to pay him he refused to take the money. He said that he was glad I had called – he had not seen a fellow countryman for many years – and invited me to call on him him whenever I had the chance. I visited him several times. The second time his daughter – a lovely girl – was there but unfortunately she spoke only French. Her parents said that when she was a small baby they spoke Slovak but when she started at school they began to speak French so that she would not be confused when learning. Now she understood their mother tongue but did not speak it.

Orders came for our unit to move. We did not know where we would go but later were told that our new posting was Bayonne, near the Spanish border. Just before we left I went to visit my farmer friend for the last time and he gave me twenty eggs for the journey.

I remembered a letter from my younger brother, Ruda, who, at the age of sixteen, was sent to a labour camp in Germany. There he was put to work on a railway line which ran through marshes; besides hunger and exhaustion, they were plagued by mosquitoes. He had written that when he said goodbye to our friends, Bohuš, Arnica, Ylya, Ondra, Natasha, Nikolai and Eda, they sent greetings to me. I knew none of these names, but remembered that under the occupation we often discussed how we could write to each other in code. One suggestion was that we would use names we didn't recognize or words out of context, and use the initial or last letter to make words. I tried linking the initial letters of these names of unknown "friends" and got the word "Bayonne." From the beginning he had insisted that we should try to keep track of each other. Now, reading it again, I realised that he was probably with the German Army in Bayonne. I hoped that I would find him there. I did not know his address as we could correspond only by a number and all letters were censored; anything considered unsuitable would be blanked out.

Our unit and horses were loaded on to a train. The wounded horses had to be transported in special wagons and once we reached Bayonne I was helping to unload them – a task that took almost two days. In our spare time when we were waiting for the wagons to come back I walked around to see if I could find the barracks where Ruda was stationed. Not far from the station was a large building with a plaque on the gate showing the number at which I used to write to him. When I asked the guard if Rudolf Novák were there he was suspicious and wanted to know how I knew this. I explained that I did not know but that the number on the gate was the number we used for correspondence, and that he was my brother. I recognized his foreign accent and asked him if he came from Silesia; he told me he was from Jablunkov. He confirmed Ruda was there and called him down to the gate.

When he came out I hardly recognized him. He was so thin – only skin and bone. He told me that the food was very poor and he was always hungry. I gave him ten eggs and a piece of bacon, which the farmer from Mauzé had given me. He was very happy – he had not tasted an egg since he had left home. We said goodbye and I went quickly back to the station because I was away without permission.

Our unit was stationed at the edge of the town. I was working in the tailoring workroom, where we had a problem. During our move the sewing-machine was damaged. The Germans had found a civilian workroom where they made a deal that I could go there to use their machine. Only two tailoresses were working there and they were always asking me questions, which I did not understand. I still knew only a few words of French so it was very difficult to converse. I was interested in the nearby mountains. I was thinking of trying to escape, but did not know where to find the border. Every time I mentioned Spain the two women were trying to tell me that this was no good. I realised afterwards that they probably sensed what I had in mind and were trying to warn me. A few days later at our roll-call it was announced that two soldiers had been sentenced to death for desertion to Spain. I think the ladies knew that the Spanish were handing back to Germany anyone they caught trying to get away, so I had to abandon the idea of escaping this way.

Shortly after this, in June 1944, Allied troops invaded Normandy. In our group everyone young enough was ordered north to join the fighting units. This time I did not try to find any excuse or mention my leg, even though it was not yet healed. About thirty of us were to go north, including the officers for whom I acted as batman. We were taken by lorry to a meeting point where there were many soldiers from different parts of France. From there we were to move on foot overnight. It was very tiring; we were marching more or less half asleep. In the morning we stopped at a small village, where we were given food – a piece of bread and some black water they called ersatz, which passed for coffee. After a few hours' sleep we were ordered to travel on. There were about two hundred of us in all. My officers told me that I need no longer look after them – they said that I would have enough to do to take care of myself. "Josef, be glad you are not German," one of them told me. "There is nothing good ahead for us."

When we were preparing to set off again I saw them putting something in their socks. Four hours later we had another break and were given a little soup. Both my officers had taken off their boots so that the first-aider could bandage their feet. Their blisters had burst and the skin was rubbed raw. Because they could not march any further they were sent to hospital. We walked all night with a break every four hours. After each rest of about half an hour it was hard to start again. We had to march overnight because aeroplanes were attacking anything on the move. The third night was the worst. Half of our group had dropped off for various reasons – stomach pains, blistered feet, any excuse not to go to the front. I too had blisters because it was difficult to march in riding boots but I bandaged myself and kept going. I **did** want to reach the front where I hoped to have the chance to get to England, though I had no idea how I would manage this. The towns we passed through were in ruins and there was a terrible stench everywhere. Maybe this was from animals or from people who had died there.

On the fourth day we reached our destination. There were now only about forty of us left; we were sitting on the grass near the woods, with no idea where we were, waiting for someone to come for us. A few minutes later we heard over the loudspeaker an announcement in German from the English, giving the Company fifteen minutes to surrender. Someone started firing a machine-gun but we did not know what to do. A quarter of an hour later all hell broke loose. Shells were falling everywhere and wounded soldiers were screaming as we started running down the road along the edge of the woods. Soon other soldiers joined us and panic reigned. The worst thing for me was that I did not know where the front or the English were, and that I was running along with Germans, with no idea where we were going. Looking for somewhere to hide I saw near the road a hole, which someone had partly covered against bombs. I climbed in, thinking that when the English arrived, I would be able to give myself up, but this hope was dashed within five minutes. "Raus!" ("Get out!") a German officer, pistol in hand, snarled at me."Ich kann nicht mehr." ("I can't do any more") I told him. "Raus!" he bellowed. He aimed his pistol at me and I thought that this was the end. I climbed out and ran like a rabbit, expecting a bullet in my back any minute. Behind me I heard a devilish laugh from the German. I ran from the woods and joined the group gathered in the fields by a farm. I was looking where I could hide because the bombs were still falling. I crawled into another hole but after about half an hour two German soldiers told me I must report to an officer they pointed out to me. As I did not belong to this unit I was quite surprised. I did not want to interrupt the officer, who was speaking to another soldier. I waited patiently but when he finished he did not even notice me. The two Germans had taken over my hole and when they began to laugh I realised that they had tricked me into moving so they could hide there themselves. The shells were still falling and I had no alternative but to look for another bolthole.

In the field there was a mound of earth about twenty metres long by a metre high. As I ran towards it, looking for another hiding place, I heard a whirring sound in the air – it sounded like a propeller. I flung myself down with my back to the mound, expecting the mine to fly past but it exploded about ten metres away from me. I felt a pain as if someone had kicked me in the stomach. In front of me I noticed a curved piece of metal about eight centimetres wide, probably from the casing of the shell. Luckily this had hit me on the flat – if it had been the edge I would not be here today. My first reaction was to pick up the metal but I promptly dropped it – it was red hot and burnt my hand.

The mines were still falling, so I jumped into the crater from the explosion. Soon afterwards I fell asleep. I woke up during the night, with a terrific thirst. My throat was dry so I went to look for something to drink. It seemed that someone was guiding me through the dark for I soon found a wooden water trough for the cows. I took a long drink and refilled my flask for the next day. The morning after, when I passed the trough, I saw that the water was green.

At the beginning of the bombardment, together with the German group we had joined, there had been about a hundred of us. By morning less than half of us were left. Many were dead or wounded and the sight of mangled bodies was horrific. My previous hiding place had taken a direct hit. Those two Germans had done me a favour by getting me out – but for their trickery I would have died in their place.

German officers were trying to restore some kind of order but the situation was chaotic. Those of us who could walk were taken to another rendezvous, where we were organized into small groups. A German Sergeant was in charge of nine of us – four young Germans, two Poles, one Yugoslav and myself. Our job was to protect the railway line. I could not see the point of this because about fifty metres away was a forest from which anyone could pick us off at any time.

The Sergeant also realised this and quickly set up a machine-gun and asked for volunteers to go into the woods to find out where the English were. The Yugoslav and I were very quick to volunteer. My companion was very young and, realising I was not German, he stuck with me all the time. The two Poles also volunteered – they were older and I did not trust them. They kept winking at me and I did not know why. They had been digging trenches somewhere when the Germans had taken them into the army.

We four went into the woods to look out for the English. I wanted to get away from the Germans and in the woods I felt safer and hoped I would have a better chance to cross to the other side. After half an hour, with no sign of any Englishmen, I told the others to wait there, where it was safer than in the open. I went back to tell the Sergeant that we were keeping watch until there was some activity to report. I had hardly finished speaking to him when my three companions came running from the woods, shouting that they could see English soldiers. The Sergeant asked how many but they were not sure, so he sent us back to try to find out. At the time I could not understand why he did not come with us. Once back in the woods I asked where they had seen the English soldiers. They told me that they had caught sight of two men on the hill to the right of the gully, where we were crouching. I left them there, where they had good cover and no one would see them, and went ahead to see if there were more English troops. To tell the truth I wanted to get closer so that I could give myself up.

I crawled towards the place they indicated and soon saw two figures lying in the grass, looking in the opposite direction. I was not sure what to do. I had a white handkerchief in my hand but was afraid that if they turned suddenly and saw me they would start shooting. I decided to take them prisoner before giving myself up. I crawled closer to them. "Hände hoch," I shouted, aiming my gun at them. To my surprise they raised their hands but when they turned round I had a terrific shock. They were German, not English. I could not imagine what would have happened if I had gone to them waving my white handkerchief.

They told me that they had been sent to help us. I think that the Sergeant, realising that we were four foreigners, did not trust us and sent the two Germans to keep an eye on us. We had turned left into the woods but they had turned right and had not been able to find us; my companions, when they saw them in the grass, naturally thought they were the English. I told these men to stay on guard where they were and report to the Sergeant if they saw any signs of activity. For our part we would keep watch to the left and report anything we saw. I went back to my companions and explained that these were German soldiers, not English. By this time it was getting dark and we decided to move further into the woods. We were going down a recently used farm track along the gully when we heard voices. It was too dark to see properly so we decided to stay where we were. Our nerves were on edge and we could not sleep but at daybreak, when we moved out of the woods, we saw a farm. The voices we had heard in the night turned out to be geese!

    The farmhouse was deserted. When we went inside there was still food on table, left by the occupants when they fled. We had had very little to eat over the past few days, and we tucked into the food hungrily; even though it was a bit dried up we did not care. After our meal, looking round the garden for somewhere to hide, I found a covered dugout big enough for ten people. There was a lot of soil on the top to protect it against bombs. Even after our sleepless night I could not rest. I was sitting near the entrance and trying to decide from which direction the firing was coming. Suddenly I noticed a group of soldiers, coming along the edge of the woods. As they drew nearer I realised they were Germans – it was our Sergeant, with about ten soldiers, yelling at us that we were surrounded. My heart leapt. I told him that we had been looking out but had seen nothing. When I said there was food in the farmhouse they immediately went inside but we stayed where we were.

Chapter 8: Five Minutes to Midnight

About half an hour later we heard the sound of an engine but we waited for it to come nearer, before showing ourselves. Our hiding place was next to a road, bordered by trees and bushes Though I was trying to find out who was coming towards us, I could not see anything through the bushes, so I left our hole, carrying my white handkerchief in my hand. As I moved quietly to the edge of the road I saw a tank beside which some soldiers were standing, talking and smoking. I could not understand them and did not recognize the uniform, so I was sure they must be English. I was moving slowly towards them, wondering how to attract their attention, when one of them turned and saw me holding up my white handkerchief. He climbed down from the tank and waved me forward with his pistol. I called to my companions that this was the English army and they could come out. The surprised soldier was looking where they came from. I told him I was Czechoslovak, the two Poles identified themselves and lastly the Yugoslav. I pointed out the farm where the Germans were eating, indicating the number on my fingers. He waved the tank towards the building and signalled that we should follow him. We were running in the direction from which the tank had come when the bombs started falling again. We quickly threw ourselves to the ground and the English officer, who was lying next to me, smiled at me and winked. I was very happy to get away from the hated Germans.

When the bombs stopped we started running again. Two hundred metres ahead we reached a small valley where there were many tanks and carriers. The Englishman took us to the command vehicle and, after a short discussion, wrote something on a piece of paper. He handed this to the driver of a carrier which we all boarded, together with another English soldier. On the way to the coast we saw many German prisoners and at the port met up with a large group of Poles and Czechs from Silesia. On the second day we sailed to England. I cannot remember the names of the

French or the English ports – I was so happy to get away from the Germans that it did not matter.

At the camp in England there were many Poles. We were told there was no Czech Army and that we should join the Polish Army. Some of the boys were ready to do this – which army did not matter as long as it was an army fighting the hated Germans. I and six other Czechs did not want this because we could not forget how the Polish had treated us when they occupied Silesia in 1939. As I looked around I saw a soldier with four silver pips on his shoulder. He was a Sergeant-Major from the Czech Army.

"Boys, there **is** a Czech Army. Can you see that Sergeant Major? He is a Czech soldier", I yelled to my friends. When they heard this, some of those who were already lining up with the Poles ran to join us. The Sergeant-Major turned when he heard me shouting in Czech and came over to us. We asked if there was a Czech Army in England as we wanted to join the fight against the Germans. He confirmed that we had an Army in the West, but he had not known that there were Czechs in the Wehrmacht. We explained that we were from Silesia, which Germany had annexed to the Third Reich. Unlike in the Protectorate of Bohemia and Moravia, where service in the German army was voluntary, all Silesian men had been called up to the German Army whether or not they wanted it. He hurried off to bring an officer, who told us that they had no idea about this situation.

From this camp we were moved to Edinburgh for screening. When they realised that I was a tailor they asked if I would be prepared to alter some uniforms in my spare time; I agreed gladly for I wanted to be useful. For this work they gave me lots of good things – chocolates and other treats which I had not tasted in years. These goodies I shared with my friends in the camp.

It was here that, during a medical inspection, one man was found to have a plaster under his arm. When the doctor removed it, instead of the sore he had been expecting he found two lightening flashes. This was the sign of the SS – the most ruthless soldiers of them all. This man was not from Silesia – he was a

German from Brno. He was immediately taken away to the prisoner of war camp. He was lucky that the other boys had not known, for they would certainly have beaten him up. We did not want to believe that the SS had tried to infiltrate us.

A fortnight later we were transferred to Southend, where we were issued with uniforms and again subjected to a medical. We from Silesia were given cover names in case we were taken prisoner. I did not even want to think about this – I would rather be dead than be taken by the Germans. It was explained that this was also for the protection of our families. I was given the name Jaroslav Bílý. I was very happy to be a soldier in the Czechoslovak Army – at last, the chance to fight for my country had become a reality.

There were about sixty young men from Silesia. When the Sergeant in charge of our group asked if we would like to attend the church service on Sunday, we all agreed. It was a beautiful day and as we marched through the town we were very proud to be wearing our Czech uniform for the first time. When we began singing our Czech marching songs people were coming out of their houses to see what was happening. Some of them joined in the procession behind us and the church was packed. After the service we sang all the way as we marched back to camp.

Our Sergeant was very surprised to see how perfectly we carried out his orders. For example, when he gave the order "Right turn" and afterwards "Halt" everything happened as one movement. He probably did not realise that most of us, even though against our will, had been in the German Army where marching was part of basic training. Back at base he told us that he had never had command of such a well-trained and well-behaved group.

At roll-call next day we felt proud when our Commanding Officer told us we were a splendid example of Czech soldiers and the whole town was talking about us. We were feeling very cheerful but we soon realised that soldiers who had been in England for a few years were complaining that we had arrived only at "five minutes to midnight". This upset us all very much because we had gone through hell to try to get away from the Germans. We had all volunteered for the Czechoslovak Army immediately we arrived in England so that we could join the fight to free our homeland. What they forgot was that when the war started most of us were only fifteen years old. In these "five minutes" which lasted almost a year, many of these young men gave their lives for their country and are buried in French and Belgian cemeteries.

At the following day's roll-call we were told to which units we would be posted. Because they started in alphabetical order, my nom de guerre, "Bílý," was the first one called. I was to be sent to a transport unit. Normally I would have been delighted. From my youngest years I had been fascinated by anything connected with cars, but I had not joined up to transport supplies; I had joined up to fight the Germans. I asked the officer in charge if I could change my posting and said I would prefer to serve in the infantry. He was very surprised as my report showed that I had a problem with my leg, but I told him that this was practically healed. He carried on down the list and found that every one of the boys wanted to change their postings and join the infantry. He stopped reading and asked the reason. To begin with there was silence – no one wanted to talk about it. When he insisted, we told him what the older soldiers were saying about our arrival at "five minutes to midnight" and that we wanted to prove that we had come to fight to ensure the speedy liberation of our country. Many of these young men did not live to see the liberation. One of those who died was my friend, Ferda, whom I had met on the train when we were called up in 1941. Because he could speak German he had stayed in Germany while I, who did not know that language, had been taken to the camp in France. When we met again in England he told me how hard his life had been in the German Army. He had escaped when his machine-gun unit (two German soldiers and himself) had been trying to trap a British contingent. Four other units had been hidden along the road and ordered to let the British troops pass through. They would then close off the road and attack from four sides. Ferda had taken the two Germans in his group prisoner and given himself up to the English, telling them where the others were waiting. The British immediately surrounded them and took them prisoner. Ferda hated the Germans and the war. He told me that if, after the war was over, a soldier marched past his house, he would lock his door and close the curtains because he did not want to be reminded of the worst time of his life. My friend fell in the fighting around Dunkirk on 5 November 1944. I will never forget him.

The officer put his list aside and simply asked those who wanted to join the infantry to step forward. Every one of us volunteered. Shortly afterwards we were posted to the motorized infantry at a tent-camp. I was standing in the front row of the new recruits waiting to be allocated to our new platoons. One of the Sergeants, Gustav Neziba, stepped forward, pointed at me and said: "I want him". He took me to a tent where he introduced me to his team and I was told to help them clean the machine-gun they were working on. These were all older soldiers with big paunches, who were taking their time over the job. When I went to help them they told me not to hurry; if they finished too quickly they would be given another job. I was disappointed for I was hoping that I would be in a group with younger soldiers. These men did not look very fit and I could not imagine how they could succeed in an attack

To begin with there were eight of us in the group – Sergeant Neziba, Lance-Corporal Lorenc, Privates Berger, Linder, Tevlovič, Tkadlec, Deneš and me. Later Privates Stařík (from Silesia) and Klimeš joined us, bringing our number up to ten. We were getting ready to move to France and a few days later we were on a ship. I was on the deck with the Sergeant when our Section Commander, Lieutenant Karnik, came along. "So, Bílý, we shall soon be in France," he said as he passed. "What do you say to that?" "It's nothing new to me," I replied. "I have been there already so I know what to expect. The worst thing is that some of our soldiers below decks don't want to go into action. They are planning how to get out of it. I am glad we are going into battle; at least it will allow those of us who turned up for the last five minutes to show our true colours." "I am sure, Bílý, that in battle every soldier will do his duty as best he can", he assured me. After he left us the Sergeant told me that the Lieutenant was worried and knew exactly what our situation was. He himself would have preferred younger soldiers but had to be satisfied with what he could get. He added that he had picked me to act as his right hand man and hoped that I would not disappoint him. "But how will Lance-Corporal Lorenc take this?" I asked him. "He is already older and he won't complain if you do some of the work for him", he assured me.

Chapter 9: The Battle for Dunkirk

After disembarkation we were told we would be engaged at Dunkirk where some fifteen thousand German troops were surrounded. Our group of thirty men was directed to take over a gun position from a Scottish unit. We travelled by lorry to within a kilometre of our post but the rest of the way we had to walk. We were carrying cases of ammunition, two soldiers to a case, and I carried a machine gun. It was dark and after we had covered half a kilometre the Sergeant asked me to check that we were all together. I discovered two of our group were missing and was sent to look for them. I soon found them sitting on their ammunition box at the side of the road. They told me the case was too heavy for them to carry. Fuming with anger, I grabbed the case, put in on my back and started running to rejoin our group. I had gone barely two hundred metres when I saw our Sergeant running towards us. He was extremely angry and began to curse them. "You pigs with big ears! Move or I'll kick your arses so hard you'll end up in hospital", he yelled. They began to run, and the Sergeant and I followed them, carrying the case.

Once back at our position, I checked again but we were still one man short. By this time the Sergeant was livid. He had to go and complete the formalities of taking over our new position but he ordered me to find the missing man. Our unit was the last to exchange positions with the Scots. I watched the Scots hurry away to board the lorries waiting for them. The last of them had left when I heard a noise in the house behind me. "Who goes there?" I shouted. (We were ordered that we must challenge in English in case the person challenged was English.) "Don't shoot! It's me", came the reply. It was Tevlovič, one of the two soldiers lagging behind earlier. I asked him what he was thinking and if he had seen the warnings of mines everywhere. He was so frightened he did not want to move. I had to lead him to join the rest of the group. The Sergeant showed us the terrain we were to guard and I was given the task of organizing the rota. We were responsible for two posts some twenty metres apart, each manned by one man, who was relieved every two hours through the night. During the day only one post was manned. When I had to choose two men to peel potatoes for our dinner the next day I picked the two who had lagged behind while carrying their ammunition box. They refused, saying that after night guard duties they were tired. "Who does he think he is?" one of them muttered as I left. "He only came at five to twelve and now he is ordering us about." By this time I had had enough and asked the Sergeant to choose someone else as his aide as I did not want the job any more. He explained that he needed me and if they would not peel potatoes they should have bread instead of potatoes for their meal.

So that they had no excuse to say I did nothing I peeled the potatoes myself, with another man to help me. At dinner-time I was waiting for them and gave them bread instead of potatoes. They were not at all happy but after that they never again refused to do kitchen duty.

Later the Sergeant called me to join him on patrol to find out exactly where the enemy positions were. I was to exclude myself from the rota as he was not sure how long this reconnaissance would take. There was a weak spot on our right wing and it was agreed that each of our three groups would provide one soldier to man this post in turn for two hours between 10pm and 4am. Before we left I had to select a man for this duty. I decided on Linder who was always grumbling. He complained bitterly that he could not do this because his sight was so poor that he should not be in the front line at all. Next morning Linder woke me up when he brought me some breakfast. I told him that I did not want anyone to do this – I could get it myself. He begged me not to send him to that post again. By this time I was getting really annoyed and gave him a good ticking off. I pointed out that as an old soldier he should set an example to us young ones instead of trying to skive all the time, and that I was only carrying out the orders of the Sergeant. After that I had no more trouble from him.

Patrols were dependent on the weather and Sergeant Neziba usually chose me to accompany him. The best time to go was when there was a moon with some cloud. In the moonlight we could see if anything moved and when the clouds came over we were able to crawl nearer to the German positions.

On our first patrol together we had a lucky escape. The moon had clouded over and we were moving very slowly, when the Sergeant told me he had kicked something. I went on my knees, telling him not to move; feeling carefully round his legs I found a wooden box, connected by a wire to another box about two metres away. We were very fortunate. We were in the middle of a minefield and if he had tripped that wire the mine would have exploded. We waited till the moon came out again and managed to get back to base by following the prints we had made in the sand.

Around Dunkirk there were thousands of mines, some left by the English in 1940 when they evacuated the area and many laid later by the Germans as a counter-measure against invasion by the Allies. There were two types – one detonated by pressure when stepped on and the other triggered by a trip wire connected to two boxes. The problem in the dunes was that in windy weather the sand was blown about covering or uncovering the mines. One day a man might safely pass over a mine buried half a metre under the sand but the next day the same mine could be on top of or only an inch or two below the surface I decided I would always crawl, feeling the ground in front of me. This way I was not only spreading my weight but the enemy had less chance of seeing me. A lot of these mines were detonated, killing and wounding many of our soldiers.

On one patrol, two other men and I had crawled through the minefield without a problem. On the way back I lay in the sand guarding our rear while my two friends, instead of crawling, were running from one dune to the next. Suddenly there was an explosion. The first man had stepped on a mine but it was the man behind him who caught the full force of explosion in his back. Luckily I was lying on the ground; if I had been running the blast would have caught me in the face. We grabbed our wounded friend and carried him back to our position. He was taken to hospital immediately but he did not survive. This need not have happened – if only they had listened to me and moved carefully the mine would not have exploded. I was lucky on these patrols, but I was always very careful. It took a little longer but it was safer.

The object of our reconnaissance was to watch for any movement in the German positions, how often they changed guard and especially to check for any sign that they were preparing to attack. We were also on the lookout for any German patrols we might be able to capture. One morning at first light, shortly after I had gone on duty, a German soldier appeared in front of our post. "Don't shoot, I am Czech", he was shouting, in our language. The alarm was raised and every man rushed to his position in case this was a trick to put us off guard. The German was ordered to keep his hands up and to move slowly towards us. When the Sergeant and I searched him to ensure he was clean, he told us he had been in No Mans Land since midnight because he did not know where the mines were laid or exactly where we were positioned. He was from Jablunkov, a town not very far from my home in Silesia, and wanted to join us to fight against the Reich. We had no option but to take him to Headquarters, where he would be interrogated before being sent on to England.

Sergeant Neziba was a very brave soldier and an excellent leader, who lived for his men. After some time at the front we were given twenty-four hours leave to go into La Panne where our Headquarters was located. When it was my turn the Sergeant mentioned that there was a very pretty waitress in the hotel where I would be staying. If she asked me if I were the brother of Gustav (himself), I should say yes. I did not understand what he meant, but had a nice surprise when about two o'clock in the morning someone came to my room and jumped into bed with me. This was the pretty waitress – and I did not sleep much that night! It was a very pleasant twenty-four hours.

The next day, as I walked through the town, a soldier greeted me. "Nazdar, kamarade. Jak se máš?" ("Hello friend. How are you?"). He was very surprised when I told him that I was OK but that I did not know him. "We were together chasing the girls in England and you don't know me?" he exclaimed. "You must be mistaken", I answered. "I have been here for a few months now." Then suddenly it struck me that he had mistaken me for my brother. Though Ruda was two years younger than me, we were very much alike. After asking a few questions I was sure he knew him. I wrote to Army Headquarters, giving details of his name, date of birth and our home address. I explained that he was my brother, and asked if they could let me know if he was in the Czech Army. Soon I received news that he was serving with the Artillery. My Commanding Officer heard about this and asked me if I would like Ruda to be transferred to our unit; if so he would try to arrange it. Friends advised me against this, telling me that if anything happened to him I would blame myself for the rest of my life, so I left things as they were. Ruda wrote to tell me that he was engaged at Dunkirk, where he was in charge of a gun. I was glad that he too had managed to escape from the Germans and that he was fighting for our country, which is what we had both wanted ever since Germany had occupied Silesia. We had had to wait a long time but our wish had at last come true.

After our twenty-four hour leave we did not get back to our post until about 11.30 at night. I should have been on patrol but because of the delay the Sergeant had taken two other men with him and I was allocated guard duty in the bunker on the 2am shift. I was lying on my bunk when a soldier ran in to tell us that there had been an explosion and volunteers were needed to bring in our wounded. Four of us grabbed stretchers and ran quickly into No Man's Land, where we saw our friends approaching – the Sergeant and another man had been wounded. I was very unhappy that I had been late – if I had been half an hour earlier perhaps there would have been no explosion. The Sergeant was sent to hospital – his left hand was injured. He was replaced by Lance-Corporal Weissberger, who was an officer cadet. Unfortunately he was not a good soldier.

On 28th October, our National Independence Day, there was a successful attack on the German positions. A further attack was planned for 5th November and this time our unit would be involved. On the 4th we were pulled back from our position to La Panne, ready to attack the following day. I visited Sergeant Neziba in hospital, told him what was happening and said that I was sorry he could not be with us. I mentioned that I did not think Lance-Corporal Weissberger, who would lead our group into the attack, was a very competent soldier. Later it turned out that I was right. I said goodbye to the Sergeant and left him at the hospital.

Shortly after midnight we boarded lorries taking us to the front, although we still did not know exactly where that was. It was still dark when we reached our rendezvous where we had to wait until daylight. Among the soldiers preparing to attack was my friend, Ferda Tichý (cover name Skala), whom I had met so many years ago on the train journey taking us to Germany. We shook hands and he told me that he had a premonition that he would not survive the battle and asked me to take his letter to his parents. We had each written a letter and given it to the other in case the worst happened. I told him not to think like this and arranged that we would get together later at a little restaurant in La Panne where we sometimes met. We said goodbye –that was the last time we would see each other.

The bombing of the German positions by allied planes at 4am was the signal for us to attack. Not long before this a dispatch rider arrived, with Sergeant Neziba sitting on the pillion. We were all surprised because he should have been in hospital. Lieutenant Karnik asked him why he had come, when he should be in hospital. "You surely don't expect to send my group into the fight without their leader", he replied quietly.

Everyone was very glad to see him, because we all liked and trusted him. We moved off through the village at a distance of about five metres from each other. The Sergeant went first; I was behind him, carrying the machine gun, and the other men followed us. Bombs and shells were falling as we moved from house to house. The Sergeant was running to the next house while I covered him; I was ready to jump to the place he had just left when I heard a noise I recognized – it was the whirring sound from a mine-thrower. I threw myself down and the mine exploded in the spot where I had been heading to. The Sergeant saw this and later asked me what made me go down instead of moving forward. I told him of my experience when I was trying to escape from the Germans and that I had recognized the sound the mine made. They fly only a short distance but you can hear them coming.

We passed through the village, mounted the tanks assembled there and started to approach the German line. We had to drive some two hundred and fifty metres across an open field and were under very heavy fire from the enemy. Because the road was so rough we were in danger of falling from the tank and getting caught in the tracks so some of us jumped down and ran next to it. When the tank stopped and started firing we threw ourselves into the ditch next to the road. Suddenly Sergeant-Major Jurník, our second in command, ran out into the field to our right, shooting. As he stopped firing, two Germans climbed out of a foxhole with their hands in the air. They were taken prisoner and sent back to the village. We were very lucky that they had been spotted. But for the Sergeant-Major's vigilance we would have taken their fire in our backs. In front of us we could see a line of German bunkers protected by rolls of barbed wire. "Bílý, to the front", I was ordered. "They need the cutters for the wire". Each group had one cutter. The sergeant told me to give the machine gun to Weissberger and go forward where there was a lot of wire. The Lance-Corporal did not want to take the gun, saying that he did not understand it, but the Sergeant rammed it into his hands. We ran quickly to the front, where the Lieutenant was waiting with two soldiers from other groups, also armed with cutters. We hit a big problem when we began to cut. Because there were several rolls of wire we had to be very careful that it did not whip back and injure us. Only one person could cut at any one time and we soon realised that it would take us too long to get through. Searching for a place with less wire, I noticed a small opening some twenty metres away. I alerted the Lieutenant, who told me to go ahead. As I crawled through the opening heavy fire was coming from a bunker to my right; to the left, from the dunes, a machine gun was pointing directly at me. I started to shoot at it, zigzagging towards it, expecting to be hit any minute, but when I got nearer I realised that the gun, probably set up to cover the blind side of the bunker, was unmanned. Had this not been the case our groups would have paid very dearly. The German guard had probably moved back into the bunker for extra protection when our tanks started shooting at their positions.

I head a faint noise and turned quickly, ready to shoot, but it was our Sergeant. As soon as the Lieutenant gave me the order to go through the gap he was right behind me. He was a terrific soldier; wounded, but heedless of the danger, he came with me. He signalled me to go for the bunker. We ran to the back entry, keeping ourselves close to the wall. I carried four English and two German grenades, one phosphor grenade and ten magazines for my sten gun. When I threw in an English grenade (which rolls) the firing immediately ceased. "Alles raus, oder ich werfe Phosphor hin!" ("Everybody out, or I throw a phosphor grenade") I yelled in my broken German. The Sergeant was at one side of the entry, I at the other, when twelve Germans filed out to surrender.

When the firing from the bunker ceased the rest of our platoon came through to join us. The Lieutenant organized a guard for the prisoners and the Sergeant told me to take the bunker to the right while he took the one to the left, and so we parted. As I ran towards the right, some of our lads were already approaching. I noticed a trench covered with camouflage, leading to the rear. I jumped down into it and, after crawling about a hundred metres, saw a light at the end of the tunnel. I wanted to fire a burst in case someone was there, but when I pulled the trigger nothing happened. I quickly moved backwards, removed the magazine and realised a bullet was jammed in the barrel. I pulled the breech a few times to knock it into place so that it would explode and clear the blockage and then replaced the magazine. Now that the gun was working properly I fired two quick bursts and jumped from the trench. In front of me I saw a half circle with five openings behind which were smaller circles, each containing a mine thrower. I had come across the mine-throwing platoon, which had been shooting at us when we were passing through the village. "Alles raus!" I was shouting, shooting into the opening. The Germans were now surrendering. I was standing with my back to the trench when I heard a movement behind me. I spun round, ready to shoot, but I recognized the helmet. It was my friend, Karel Berger, a member of our group. Before the attack Karel had asked me if I were strong enough to carry him. When I asked why he told me that he was Jewish and worried he would be taken prisoner by the Germans. I assured him that I did not want to be taken either and promised I would not leave him behind if he were wounded, even though I would have to drag him – he was a very heavy man.

When he saw me going into the trench he had followed me. I was glad because there were quite a lot of Germans giving themselves up. "Hände hoch!" I was shouting all the time. An officer approached, his hands by his sides, demanding to speak to one of our officers, but when I sent a burst over his head he stopped immediately and raised his hands. Had he not done so I would have let him have it because I would not trust a German. I was glad Karel was there – had they realised I was alone God knows what would have happened.

Instead of letting our prisoners go along the trench we made them climb up the wall to the top of the dugout, where our men were waiting to take over. I was very surprised when Karel started to yell at them in perfect German. I told him to stay there with them while I went ahead to reconnoitre. The trench led further back but without camouflage. I had gone only a hundred metres when I heard machine-gun fire. I ducked but realised the firing was not towards me. I looked round to see where this fire was coming from and soon spotted three men with a machine gun, firing towards our men. I came out of the trench behind them and crawled forward, ready to fire if they saw me. When they stopped to replace the ammunition belt I was ten metres away. I fired a burst over their heads, yelling "Hände hoch!." They very quickly obeyed. As I ordered them away from the gun one of them bent down to pick up a bag. Again I fired a burst in the air, shouting at him to drop the bag, which he did. When he turned to look at me I had the shock of my life. He looked just like my father – small, with a moustache, about fifty years old. It was frightening to realise that I could have shot my own father who, as a railway worker, could easily have been taken into the German Army. I ordered our captives to go along the top but I stayed in the trench, where I was partly protected if there were more Germans around. I took them to join the rest of the prisoners – there were quite a lot of them by this time.

Before the attack we were told that we would have backup to disarm the enemy weapons. As there was as yet no sign of them I went back to the mine throwers. I dropped one of my German grenades into the barrel of the first gun, sprinted to the next one and did the same thing, but had time only to throw an English grenade at each of the other three nests as my first grenades were already exploding. One of these explosions was much louder than the rest – I think the grenade hit mines the enemy had ready to fire. I ran from the trench as our platoon was moving out with the prisoners. I was going to join them when I saw Sergeant Neziba, looking very tired, leaning on the wall of the bunker. Round his neck he had a gun belt and binoculars, which he had taken from enemy soldiers. When I asked, he said he was OK but I could see that he could barely stand. I signalled a passing carrier, which took him aboard to get him back to the hospital, and then I rejoined my unit. After handing over the prisoners we climbed on to the lorries to return to La Panne. We cleaned ourselves up before going into town to the little pub to meet our friends from the other groups. We were talking about our experiences in the battle, saddened by the news that our casualties were very heavy. Most of them were in the area where my friend, Ferda, had been fighting. We waited but our friends did not come. There was a sudden commotion in one corner. One of our soldiers was yelling that there were some German soldiers wearing Czech uniforms. He pointed out two men sitting in the corner. They protested that this was untrue – they were Czech soldiers and had papers to prove this, but their accuser insisted that as they were speaking German their IDs might be forged. Things were looking very bad for this pair, especially after a battle where we had lost so many comrades, until fortunately one of our soldiers recognized them. We were all upset that these two men, who had not been involved in the action, were speaking German. I remembered a similar incident at our post.

One night the Sergeant and I had returned from patrol about 1am and while he went to report I went to check the guards. When I heard voices by the first post I lay down because where there should have been only one man on duty there were two and I was shocked to realise that they were speaking German. The first thing that sprang to mind was that the Germans had managed to get into our position. I looked round to see if I could see more of them. I was prepared to shoot as I crawled slowly towards them. "Hände hoch", I yelled, when I was a few metres away from them. Their hands shot up – if they had not I would certainly have shot them. To my relief I recognized two of our men, one of whom had left his post to talk in German with his friend. I cursed them both because, thinking they were the enemy, I had nearly killed them. I was also furious with the one who had left his post, pointing out that if I could get so close undetected so could the enemy. Though they begged me not to report them I felt I had to tell the Sergeant; we all had to be able to depend on each other and know that each was doing his duty conscientiously. I wondered what would have happened if I had shot them, and found it hard to understand why Jews still preferred to speak in German, despite the atrocities against their people by the Nazis.

I waited a long time for Ferda but when he did not turn up at the pub I realised that I would not see him again. The following day I heard that he and his entire group had been killed. I was very sad, for we had become very good friends.

After this action we were given a few days leave. Two men from our platoon were wounded – one was our Commanding Officer, Lieutenant Karnik, a very good commander, who led his men from the front and had earned our respect. Our new commander was Lieutenant Opočenský. Sergeant Neziba had gone back to the hospital and Lance-Corporal Weissberger had taken his place. As I have said before, the latter was not a very good soldier. During the attack no-one saw him anywhere and he had become my enemy when the Sergeant had thrown the machine-gun to him so that I could help cut the barbed wire. He still blamed me that he had had to carry the gun.

On the second day after the battle our company went on a marching exercise through the town. The column was led by the Commanding Officer, followed by the Group Commanders, the machine-gunners, of which I was one, and the rest of the men, carrying rifles, brought up the rear. Weissberger, our Group Commander, had a Sten gun, which he ordered me to carry for him. I refused, telling him that I was not his batman. When he ordered me to the back of the column I replied that I could only leave my place on the authority of the Senior Officer who was leading us. He was furious. "Just wait; I'll show you!" he snarled. When we returned from this march I was called before the Lieutenant, who told me that the penalty for disobeying a direct order from the Lance-Corporal would be peeling potatoes instead of having a free afternoon. He did not give me the chance to explain what happened. Nor was this the end of the matter. I was due to take driving lessons but this chance was now given to someone else. My friends were very surprised when they saw me doing kitchen duty because I was usually the one who allocated the jobs to others.

Soon after we returned to the frontline the Company Commander, Captain Kronek, arrived at our position. He called me to the office and told me that I had been chosen to lead a large patrol from Headquarters. In the past I had always volunteered for patrol duty but after the way they had treated me I did not want to go. I asked him whether this was an order or whether it was voluntary; when he confirmed that it was voluntary, I declined. He was very surprised, as I had always been the first to volunteer for any patrol. When he asked for a reason I hesitated because I was not sure whether I should tell him what had happened. I was quiet for a while and kept looking at the Lieutenant, and then said I had my reasons but did not want to talk about it. The Captain realised something was wrong and asked the Lieutenant to leave us. When he left he snapped: "What happened? Out with it!" I told him everything. He looked at me in disbelief but he told me that I did have a very good reason to refuse his request and he would try to find someone else. When I was leaving him I stopped outside the door for a minute and I heard him telling the Lieutenant off, saying he did not deserve to be a commander if he did not know the soldiers under his command. I did not listen any longer. I ran back to grab my jacket, which I had adapted specially for the patrols. I had stitched extra pockets to hold six magazines, so divided that they didn't touch each other because, at night, even the slightest rustle is audible. I dressed quickly and ran back to the jeep to wait. A few minutes later the Captain came and when he saw me waiting he smiled. "I knew you wouldn't let me down," he said.

There were ten men in this patrol, led by a Sergeant-Major; the rest were volunteers from Headquarters, including two English soldiers with a machine-gun. They were seconded to our infantry for training as they were previously members of the RAF ground force. The object of our patrol was to bring back enemy prisoners. I was afraid that there were too many of us for this task; I told the Captain that two or three would be plenty and I knew the place where we could succeed. The Captain felt as I did but the patrol was sent from Headquarters and there was nothing he could do about it. I was sorry that Sergeant Neziba was not with us. I tried to explain to the Sergeant-Major how we could achieve our object. The enemy had a lookout manned by one man, well in front of the line. This guard was changed every two hours. I suggested that I could approach the post from the left side while he came from the right. If either of us were spotted, the other would engage the guard. The rest of our men would have to stay back so that they would not inadvertently alert the guard by any small noise they might make. Earlier Sergeant Neziba and I had worked out this method and found it effective. With so many men it would be very difficult to pass safely through the minefield. I pointed out that we must crawl one behind the other; I could lead the way along a route I had used before. As we neared the German position the English soldiers were having problems with the machine-gun. We really did not need that gun and every time it touched a bush or anything it made some slight noise and in the night sound travelled a long way.

We finally managed to get below the post where we wanted to take our prisoners. Now we could use only hand signals. I signalled to the Sergeant-Major that I would go left as first suggested and he should go to the right. I had to pass between two dunes to reach the side of the guard post. I ran a few steps and flung myself down when a rifle was fired in my direction. I lay there, waiting for the Sergeant-Major to engage the guard. As soon as the guard began shooting in the opposite direction I could get into his position, which was only about five metres away.

I waited but, when I looked back, was horrified to see the Sergeant-Major and the rest of the patrol retreating, but instead of going towards our own line they were heading straight for the enemy. I started running to stop them when another shot went past me and I knew that any moment all hell would break loose. I managed to catch them, explained they were heading in the wrong direction and that the Germans would be sending up flares and shooting, so we would be very lucky to get out of there alive. The unfortunate thing was that it was not the Germans shooting at us – it was our own side. The Sergeant-Major had radioed back to base to ask for covering fire but, because by then we were already in the German lines, it was aimed at us. Luckily we were, by then, clear of the dunes and it was passing over our heads. It is difficult to run in sand and we arrived back completely exhausted, especially the two men carrying the heavy machine-gun. We were very lucky that none of us was wounded by this friendly fire. We were also fortunate that no one stepped on a mine, for we had to run regardless of the danger.

When we went to report, the Sergeant-Major insisted that we were discovered; when he saw me hit the ground he thought I was dead and had given the order to retreat. The Captain dismissed him but ordered me to stay; he asked me what really happened. I told him everything but added that the real problem was that there had been too many of us and the guard must have heard us coming. We were fortunate that there were no more of the enemy waiting for us or we would not have escaped with our lives. If the Sergeant-Major had done as I had suggested when the German was shooting at me, he could have surprised him from behind and taken him prisoner. Instead he had panicked and started retreating.

A few days later another patrol went out from our platoon – a corporal and two soldiers – to occupy an empty bunker nearer the German line and to observe German movements. The mistake they made when they moved in during the night was that they had left a trail of footprints in the sand, leading towards the bunker, not away from it. When the Germans realised it was occupied they tried to recapture it, but fortunately it was under our observation and every time the enemy approached we drove them back with machine-guns and mine-throwers. After dark we went in to help them evacuate safely.

I received some bad news. Lieutenant Karnik and Sergeant Neziba had nominated me for promotion to Lance-Corporal but unfortunately they were no longer with us. Lieutenant Opočenský and Lance-Corporal Weissberger countermanded this and gave the promotion to someone else. I think Lieutenant Opočenský realised afterwards that he had been unfair because when news came from Headquarters that the Group Leader could nominate one soldier for a three-day holiday in Paris, he suggested me and off I went. The Lieutenant had some family in Paris and asked me if I could deliver a parcel to them, which I gladly did. I travelled to the address by metro. On the way back, as I waited for the train, I heard two girls speaking Czech behind me. "Je to Čech, nebo ne?" ("Is it Czech, or isn't it?") one of them asked her companion. "Ano, je Čech!" ("Yes, it is Czech!") I replied, turning towards them. I was surprised to hear my own language in France. The girls had noticed the "Czechoslovakia" flash on my shoulder and were wondering if I really was a Czech soldier. I was glad I met them because they showed me around Paris, which they knew very well. I have very happy memories of my three days' leave.

Back with my unit I went on patrol with two men from another group. One of them, Acel, was a Slovak who believed that what is meant to happen in one's life will happen, no matter what one does. He believed that somewhere a candle was burning for him and that when it went out his life would end. The second man was from the Government Army. (This was a group of men from the Protectorate who had volunteered for the German Army but, when they were sent to the Italian front, had walked across to the Allies and given themselves up so they could join the Free Czechoslovak Army.) He was older and had a wife and family at home in Czechoslovakia. When I explained how carefully we must proceed because of the many mines they did not take me seriously. I led, they followed; we moved very carefully, crawling most of the time. On the way back Acel went first and I brought up the rear. I was lying by a sand dune, covering our rear, and my friends were running from dune to dune, even though I had warned them how dangerous this was. Suddenly there was a loud explosion and the second man caught the full force of the blast in his back. Luckily I was lying flat, and protected by the dune. We were very close to the enemy line. I jumped up and ran to help Acel drag our wounded companion towards our post. There they had heard the explosion and a stretcher party was already on its way to help us. As we carried him he cursed the Germans and life in general and asked us to tell his wife and children that he loved them. His back had been badly damaged by shrapnel and he died on the way to hospital. "Your candle didn't go out, but his did", I told Acel later. "It was your fault. If you had been careful this would never have happened. Now at home those kids have lost their father."

After our dying comrade was taken away and we had been debriefed I felt a strange tiredness. The Lieutenant asked if I was all right and then looked at my legs and asked if I was hurt. I told him I was OK, but he looked again and told me I was bleeding.

On patrol I always wore Canadian leather high-laced boots because the sand did not get into them. When the mine exploded I had been lying on the other side of a dune which had protected me from the blast but my legs must have been sticking out. A small piece of shrapnel had caught me even though I had not felt it. When the boot came off it did not look too bad; the leather had protected me a bit. The bleeding was caused by a few slivers of shrapnel. After having it dressed I rejoined my platoon.

To celebrate the birthday of our late first President, Tomáš Garrigue Masaryk, on 7th March I was called to our Headquarters in La Panne, where I received an award for bravery.

What made me especially happy was seeing that many of the soldiers who received medals alongside me were from Silesia. It proved that in the "five minutes to midnight" they had excelled themselves in the fight against the Germans.

Chapter 10: The Disappointment of the Liberation of the Homeland

In April 1945 a detachment of 140 Czechs, led by Major Sitek, left the troops besieging Dunkirk to join up with the 3rd US Army. When they crossed the border into Czechoslovakia on 1st May they raised our national flag at Cheb.

On 8th May, at 8.30 am, our Czech Commandant sent an ultimatum to Vice-Admiral Frisius, the German Officer in Command at Dunkirk, ordering him to present himself at our Headquarters. Although he was not happy to do this, the Admiral had no alternative and he signed the document of unconditional surrender on the morning of 9th May. The Czechoslovaks took fifteen and a half thousand German prisoners and seized three U-boats.

The war in Europe was finally over and on 12th May we started our journey home. The first day on the road we infantrymen were resting on the grass verge when a column of artillery passed by. I was looking to see whether my brother was among them. I had given up hope when suddenly, as the last gun came round the bend, I saw him standing next to the driver. When I called out his name he turned round and waved to me, but they were hurrying after the others and could not stop.

Later, when we stopped for the night, I went to see him and we talked together of our experiences. He told me how he had escaped from the Germans through the woods from France to Italy and then showed me a present he was taking for our father. It was a kitbag full of cigarettes; he did not smoke but had saved his ration, as I had. I told him my kitbag was also full of cigarettes. Father was a very heavy smoker and throughout the occupation, when cigarettes were rationed, he had been very unhappy.

At last we arrived in our homeland. Once, when we were resting, my friends were sitting on the grass by the road while I was in our half-track making sandwiches. "Jardo, for Heaven's sake hurry up! I'm dying of hunger," one of the boys called to me.

A woman, who heard this as she was passing by, asked who we were. When we told her we were the Czech Army she did not believe us - she said that Czechs did not look like us. When I looked at my friends I knew she was right – we had spent several days on the road in the scorching hot sun and we were sunburned and dirty. After I showed her the Czech Lion and the word "Czechoslovakia" on my sleeve she was convinced and dashed off across the fields to tell her family.

As we drew nearer to Plzen more and more people were lining the road. Suddenly one of our men jumped down and ran to give somebody a hug – he had recognized his parents in the crowd.

Our motorized infantry unit spent one night in the town of Klatov, before being sent to the village of Vojovice, where the people gave us a wonderful welcome. When we arrived in our halftracks we were greeted by a brass band and girls wearing national dress, carrying bunches of flowers, one for each soldier. After the welcoming speeches we went to the local pub where they had prepared refreshments for us. Such a spread we had not seen for a long time. The place was packed with locals; the band played and we were dancing the whole night through. This was a beautiful celebration and I think of it often.

Our job in Vojovice was to look out for enemy soldiers trying to get back to Germany now the war was over. The area round the village was constantly patrolled. We positioned our halftrack at the edge of the woods where we could observe the main road. One lunchtime, as we were preparing to have a snack, two German soldiers came out of the bushes with their hands up; they had been hiding in the trees during the day and at night were walking in the direction of Germany, but when they saw that we had food they decided to surrender as they had not eaten for a few days. They begged for something to eat and were very grateful for the bread and ham we gave them. I could not help remembering how badly we had been treated by their fellow countrymen when we were hungry. They were taken to Headquarters, from where they were sent to a prison camp.

Our Army had been deployed in Belgium, but my comrades and I had wanted to help liberate Prague. There the people had risen up against the Germans when they had learnt that the American Army had advanced to within a hundred miles, and they had been calling desperately for help. A frustrated General Patton and his troops were forced to halt after liberating Plzen on 6th May. They were forbidden to cross the demarcation line agreed by Churchill, Roosevelt and Stalin at the Yalta Conference. Only the Russians were to liberate Prague. We found it difficult to understand what right politicians had to decide in advance who would free our capital city. We had always hoped that we would be helping the fight in our country but we were denied this right because of some political decision. The politics of keeping Stalin happy were apparently more important than the lives of the people. We took that very badly. The Red Army reached Prague on 10th May, but many of those who had so bravely risen up against the Nazis were killed before they arrived. Russia was also given the greatest say in the formation of the new government.

Our units were finally allowed into the city but only to take part in the parade of the Western Army. We were billeted on the White Mountain, where a unit of Czechs who had fought on the Eastern Front was stationed. These men were ill-equipped and poorly dressed – their uniform consisted of a shirt worn outside their trousers, held in at the waist with string. They eagerly accepted cigarettes from us, telling us how envious they were of our equipment and our smart uniforms.

We were given a day off before the big parade. As we strolled through the streets we realised that none of our compatriots had any idea that there had been a Czech Army in the West.

Before the start of the parade, President Beneš thanked the soldiers for their efforts and added that the Army would still be needed to help re-build the new Czechoslovakia. Thousands turned out to cheer us as we marched. Flags were waving and everyone was so happy. This is a good memory.

Once the parade was over we were disappointed that we were ordered to return immediately to Plzen. It was obvious that those in authority did not want us in Prague.

In the meantime I managed to get a place on a course in stock control for automobile spare parts, which was being organized in Nepomuk. I wanted to stay in the army and any training or qualification of this type would be very useful in our motorized unit. When I had completed the course I rejoined my unit in Vojovice.

Later our company moved to Česka Lípa, where new recruits joined us for training. I was transferred to a technical unit and promoted to sergeant. The man in charge of our platoon, Warrant-Officer Pěčontka, came from Sub-Carpathian Russia and had been transferred to us from the Eastern Army. Our duties included looking after our army vehicles, confiscated German cars and stores of spare parts, which were guarded day and night.

When someone stole one of our English Bedford trucks we interrogated the guards but could not find out how it could have happened. I was the Warrant-Officer's deputy and he assured me that he would find out who had committed this crime. The next day I heard a noise in the corridor outside the office and went out to see what was happening. I was surprised to see eight Russian soldiers guarded by one of the recruits, who had a rifle in his hand. He told me that they had been brought in by Warrant Officer Pěčontka, who was questioning a Russian officer. The young soldier complained that the Russians were pushing him about and he did not know what to do, as he was not allowed to shoot at them. I grabbed his bayonet, fixed it to his rifle and told him he did not need to shoot but if one of them came near him he could stick it in him to show him how things stood. The Russians looked at me sullenly when I told them to stand in the corner of the passage, as otherwise I would not guarantee their safety. About ten minutes later I could stand the suspense no longer; I went out to check what was happening. All was quiet – my soldier told me that he was having no problems with his charges, so I went to the office to find out what this was all about.

Pěčontka was standing in the centre of the room with a smile on his face; he told me he knew where the truck was, to whom and for what it had been sold. In the corner on the floor was a Russian officer with a bloodied face. Pěčontka had beaten him until he confessed where the truck had gone and now he ordered me to bring a car and a few soldiers. We were going to pick up the stolen vehicle, which was in Bory, not far from Česka Lípa. We found our truck and arrested the civilians who had bought it for a few bottles of alcohol. I asked the Warrant-Officer if I should report the incident but he told me that he would attend to it. The next day three jeeps carrying high-ranking Russian officers arrived, asking to see Captain Kronek, our Company Commander. Shortly afterwards he called me into his office to ask who had questioned the Russian officer. When I told him, he asked me to take the visitors to Warrant-Officer Pěčontka, who would explain to them what had happened. Pecontka was smiling as they went into his office. I waited in the passage, wondering what would happen. A quarter of an hour later the door opened. The Russian officers were saluting our Warrant-Officer, who returned the salute with a smile. It surprised me that such high-ranking officers would salute an NCO, who could not even write his name properly. There was something wrong if a junior officer had more power than those of higher rank. We never heard any more about this episode.

There was another incident involving the Russians. A soldier from the Western Army and a policeman were visiting a lady, when somebody smashed the glass door and started shooting at them with a sten gun. The soldier was sitting on the settee while the lady was pouring coffee by the table. The policeman had managed to pull his pistol only halfway from his holster when the bullets hit them. The only survivor was a two-year-old girl, who was playing in the corner of the room.

We were on the scene in minutes, to be greeted by a horrific sight. The flat was a shambles, smashed by the bullets; the terrified child was huddled in the corner and the three adults were dead. Neighbours reported that they had recognized a

Russian soldier running away after the shooting. He had tried a few times to form a relationship with this lady but she had turned him down. When the Russians were asked to hand him over to us they refused, insisting that he was a German wearing a Russian uniform, whom they believed to be a spy. He had already been taken away for questioning.

In our Company we had been ordered not to carry weapons but after this unfortunate episode we began taking with us any small arms still in our possession. Once, on a short cut from the railway station to the town, three Russians, walking abreast, met three of our soldiers, who were walking in the opposite direction. They met in the middle and neither side wanted to give way. The Russians wore their guns on the back but our boys noticed they were pulling them to the front into the firing position and realised what they had in mind. One Czech soldier began shooting through his pocket. They were so close to each other that he hit all three Russians in the stomach or the side and they went down, two seriously wounded and one slightly wounded. Witnesses said that the man shooting was from the Western Army – they recognized his black beret. There was an investigation but without result. I found out by accident who the culprit was. I was in charge of sleeping quarters shared by twenty six men and during my inspection the day after the shooting I came across a soldier who should not have been there. We all had a job to do but he told me he had the day free because he had been on guard through the night. He was acting very suspiciously. I approached his bed and when I picked up the overcoat lying there I noticed a hole burnt through the pocket. He had tried to put a patch over it but not very successfully. He explained that if he had not stopped the Russians he and his friends would have been shot. I told him I was a tailor and offered to mend the coat for him, but even though I made a good job of it, the repair was still visible under close inspection. I took it to our warehouse and exchanged it for another one. I did not report this because I knew he had shot in self-defence. All the Russians survived.

Many of our Western soldiers were leaving the army but a few of us were waiting to be accepted by the Army Academy. When we were engaged at Dunkirk Captain Kronek had asked if I would like to enter the Officer Training Academy. He would recommend me for this as I had a lot of fighting experience. I accepted his offer gladly. However, now the war was over, we were told the Academy was full and we would have to wait a further two years before we could be accepted. If we were agreeable they would, in the meantime, give us the rank of Warrant-Officer. I refused because I thought two years was too long to wait, but some of the men accepted these terms. After waiting for two years, instead of entering the Academy they were arrested. In the summer of 1946 I left the army with the rank of sergeant. During my time in the service I had been awarded the Military Medal, the Czech War Cross, two medals for bravery, a good conduct medal, two campaign medals (France/Germany and the 1939/1945 Star) and the Victory Medal.

I was glad to be with my family again. I learnt that, after I left in 1941, Marie had been drafted into a labour camp at Auschwitz, in Poland, where she had to work without pay. She told us that conditions were very bad, but what she remembered most was the awful smell from the crematorium in the Jewish camp. Later she was taken as a maid to a German family and moved to Germany. Though she did not enjoy working there it was better than in the camp. Leoš, who now had three sons, was still in the police force.

Emilie and Marie were engaged to be married and I was happy to help finance these two weddings. Anna was still working in the cake shop and Eliška, my youngest sister, had left school and was helping my mother.

Back in civilian life once more, I began looking for work. As I had completed only two years' training in my youth I would have to work as an apprentice for another year if I wanted to become a tailor. I needed money and found a job as a lorry driver but unfortunately this lasted for only one day. On my first day at work I was surprised to learn that the driver of the lorry was

German and I was expected to shovel sand to fill the truck for him. This I refused to do and I left. I decided to do a course at business school, which would give me a chance to do office work. After finishing my studies I got a job with the State Health Insurance. In the beginning I worked in the office, but later I was accepted for a post as an inspector. This work was outside the office and involved a lot of travelling but this did not worry me. If a patient was sick for more than a fortnight I had to visit him or her to check whether the case was genuine. Often, especially in the summer when there was plenty of work in the gardens and fields in the villages, people would stay at home to help, while claiming sickness benefit. Later, when a position as stock controller in the dental stores became vacant, I took this job. Here they kept the supplies of drills, materials for dentures, etc, but there was a problem in the storeroom, where it was taking too long to process the orders from the dentists. The Director of the Insurance Office, who knew that I had had experience of storekeeping and stock control, wanted me to reorganize the system so that things would move more quickly. When I started the job it was taking about two hours to complete an order, but when I completed the changeover to the system we had used in the army we were managing to get the orders out in ten to fifteen minutes. Because the whole process was now much quicker I had a lot of spare time so I took on another job as driver of the Director's official car. Besides work in the store I drove him to official meetings.

Chapter 11: Five Minutes to Midnight
- the second time

Since the end of the war the Communist Party, together with the Trade Unions, had become increasingly powerful and in 1946 was the largest party in the coalition government. Klement Gottwald became Prime Minister, but as their popularity waned he realised that the Communists had no chance of winning a fair and democratic election. In February 1948 he launched a well organized coup, using the workers' militia and the Communist dominated police; in June he took over the Presidency from Eduard Beneš and began the Stalinization of the country. People were encouraged to spy on their neighbours and to inform the police of any potentially anti-Communist behaviour; they were persuaded to report members of their own families for anything which might be construed as anti-party or anti-state. In every workplace and apartment block there was someone, watching and listening, who would relay to the authorities everything that was going on. Distrust was corrosive and all-pervasive.

In July 1948 the Director of Social Services, who often accompanied the Director to meetings, came to see me. She was a very pleasant lady and we got on well together. She was obviously very upset. "Joe, I need help", she told me. "My son, Radek, was studying in Brno but after the coup he left for Germany, where he was in a refugee camp. He came back for financial help. He has been staying with his grandfather in Brno but his brother, who is a Communist, reported him to the authorities and they are looking for him." The boy had left Brno and come to stay with her in Těšin but she was afraid that the police would come there to look for him. I told her that we lived in a village near the forest and that her son could stay with us for a while, for which she was grateful.

When I went to her flat to pick up Radek, I told him to lie on the floor in the back of the car so that no one would see him. Once at my house he agreed he would not go outside unless he saw someone coming down the lane, in which case he would run and hide in the woods, which were only a few metres from the house.

Before the war I had become a member of the Sokol Club when I was seven years old, as had my younger brother, Ruda. After leaving the army in 1946 we decided to start our local club again and soon had a hundred and fifty members, of whom sixty were active. I was in charge of the active members. Poles, who hated Sokol because it was a club of Czech patriots, were still a problem.

After the coup in February the Government set up National Councils throughout the country, the members of which were all Communists. All other political parties were banned. One Friday evening at the end of August I was called before the Council in our village. Most of the members were Polish, as was the Chairman, who began to question me in his own language. I told him I did not understand and asked him to speak Czech; I pointed out that as we were in Czechoslovakia he should speak our language. He stopped talking and ordered his Polish deputy to question me. This man had some documents in front of him and he said they had received a complaint that, at a Sokol reunion in Prague, I had shouted anti-government slogans. I replied that I had not been in Prague because my employers refused to give me time off from work. They were taken aback because they had no answer to that. After further hunting through the documents they brought up another point on which they needed clarification. They wanted to know why in the Army I had attained the rank of sergeant so quickly and why I had so many medals. This question surprised me but I told them that I had been a good soldier and the medals were for things I had done under fire, all recorded at Army HQ. They then accused me of attending a course in anti-socialist politics. I could not remember any such a course. I stated that I was a patriot who had risked his life to free his country and that I was very upset to be accused of acting against the Czech state. I reminded them that most of the Committee members were Poles. They had invaded our country, bearing arms, in 1938, and **this** was action directed against the State. "I don't know what right you have to question me," I repeated. When I mentioned 1938 I could see they did not like it. There were no more questions but they told me that my next interrogation would be by the police.

The next day, Saturday, on my way to work to prepare urgent orders needed by dentists for Monday morning, I met an old friend who was in the police force. I was stunned to hear that a warrant had been issued for my arrest; I had no idea that I had done anything wrong. When I asked him what the charge was he told me that on the warrant were written the words "Not to be trusted." I wondered how they had managed to obtain a warrant in so short a time; it looked like it had been ready and waiting to be served. He warned me that I had the weekend free but I would certainly be arrested on the Monday.

Instead of going to work I called on another policeman, a friend of my older brother, Leoš. After the February putsch he had told me at one of our Sokol meetings that if I ever needed assistance I could go to him. When I explained what had happened he was more than willing to help me. He knew of someone in Asch, a town near the Czech-German border, who, for Kr. 2000, would take me across the border into Germany. I accepted this offer because freedom was better than jail.

There were many valuable items in the dental storeroom so I had to arrange to leave the keys in safe hands. I went to see another friend who had been in the Western Army and whom I had helped to get a job in the insurance office. He promised to give the keys to the Director, and to no one else. The reason I gave was that I had to go away for a few days on family business. I told my mother I must leave and that my friend, Radek, would be going with me. I said goodbye to her but my father was working. I was sorry to leave without seeing him.

At midnight, we left Těšin for Prague, where we boarded a train to Asch. My policeman friend, who was on the same train, told us to follow him but under no circumstances must we contact him. As we were about to leave the train we noticed that police were checking everyone's papers. Luckily we were in the last carriage and were able to get off the train on the opposite side, where nobody saw us. We walked back along the line in the direction from which we had come and once we came to a more shadowy spot crossed the track, jumped over a fence and managed to get to the road. Our policeman friend was waiting when we got back to the station, very relieved that we had avoided the control where several people had been arrested.

We followed him into town and waited in the street when he disappeared into one of the houses. A few minutes later another man emerged, came straight to us and told us to go with him. By this time it was again midnight and taking us by the shoulders he began to sing. When I asked why he was making so much noise he told me we should pretend we were going home from the pub, drunk. I did not agree with him. For one thing we were walking towards the border and, if challenged, would have to explain why we were carrying luggage. He was half-drunk and refused to go any further but showed us which direction to take. Pointing across the fields, he told us that about half a kilometre ahead we would pass a swimming pool, now closed. It was just before the railway – once we had crossed the line we would be in Germany. With that, he turned and left us.

Radek could not remember the area because it had been dark when he had left Germany on his way back home. All we could do was follow the directions of our guide. It was dark and we had no idea where we were. As we moved forward very carefully along the bushes bordering the field it reminded me of our patrols in Dunkirk. I decided it was better to go slowly in case border guards were about. Eventually we reached the swimming pool and moved even more carefully. We waited for about half an hour before going on, in case any guards were lurking in the chalets by the pool. We moved cautiously from one building to the next and about an hour later we saw the railway. We waited a bit longer but as everything was quiet we decided it was safe to cross.

The railway track ran about two metres above the field and as we began to run up the gravel bank, we started to slip. We were only about a hundred metres away from one of the border posts and the racket we made soon had men with barking dogs hurrying to investigate. It seemed to take us ages to get to the top. On the other side it was easier; we more or less slid down on our behinds. As soon as we reached firm ground we had to run about two hundred metres across a field and we were at last in Germany. Looking back towards the guard post we could see men and dogs trying to locate the source of the noise.

Radek recognized this place. He told me that on this side of the border, opposite the Czech guard post, was the home of a Czech family, who would let us stay in their house till next morning. He had stayed with them overnight when he was returning home from Germany. These people gave us food and allowed us to stay the night. We left them next morning to catch the bus to Selb, where we were met by German police as we got off. They had received a report of a disturbance near the border and were waiting for the first bus of the day. In this area the police force operated under American control and we were taken to US Army Headquarters. The German policeman remembered seeing Radek in the town a month previously and reported that we were spies.

An American officer, helped by another soldier, was searching our belongings when he found my citation, written in English, for the Military Medal I had been awarded during the war:

"*Private Jaroslav Bílý*

During an offensive action on 5th November 1944, Private Bílý observed heavy mortar fire concentrated on his own unit. With another man he stalked the enemy mortar position with complete disregard for his personal safety and forced the surrender of the entire enemy mortar platoon, together with the officer commanding. This was a fine example of great coolness and tactical skill."

(Jaroslav Bílý was my cover name when I was in the army.)

He read this and asked if it were mine. I knew enough English to understand him and answered in the affirmative. He ordered the other man to put all our belongings back, stood up, shook my hand and saluted me. He said something else, which I did not understand. "Alles in Ordnung," he told the German policeman. The German was nonplussed; he had no idea what was written in my documents or why the American was saluting me. The Americans gave us travel documents to a camp at Regensburg, the first screening point for political refugees. Radek had already been through this camp and thought it would save a lot of time if we by-passed it and carried on to Ludwigsburg where he was registered.

When we arrived there it was fine for him but I was sent back to Regensburg, where, after questioning, I was given papers as a political refugee. This camp was packed with refugees; we were forty to a room. From the very beginning I had been warned not to say where I had crossed the border and who had helped me. No one could be trusted. The Communists were already infiltrating the refugee camps, trying to find out where and how refugees were escaping and who was helping them. I heard that someone working in the camp office used to listen in to the interrogation sessions, making notes of everything he heard. Later he disappeared, taking all this information with him.

A week later I was sent to the Ludwigsburg camp, where I met Radek again. He took me to a room shared by thirty people, and introduced me to his companions, telling them we had come across the border together and that I had been a soldier in the Western Army. I dumped my things on the bed and went for a shower. While I was away there was quite a debate about me. Among them was a young man who said he had been a Lieutenant in the Western Army, engaged at Dunkirk, and he insisted anyone could make this claim. Radek told them how the American officer had reacted when he checked my credentials. He could not tell them what was written on the paper; when he had asked me I had told him only that they were army documents. They insisted he should look in the envelope where I kept them, so that they could all see them. There I had my English and Czech decorations and my army pay book. One of the students who spoke a little English translated the citation for them. In my pay book I had kept my invitation to the British Embassy in Prague where I had been presented with the Military Medal. The ribbon was blue and white; the medal itself bore the head of the King on one side, on the other was written "For Bravery in the Field", and around the edge of the medal was engraved my name. My other medals were also in the envelope. They asked the Lieutenant if this were proof enough and if he could produce any military documents to back up his claim, but he told them he had not had time to collect his papers before he had had to leave Czechoslovakia.

When I went back into the room everybody was very quiet and I asked what had happened. The Lieutenant told me what Radek had said about our interview by the American officer. My friend apologised for looking in the envelope to see what the American had read but I told him not to worry as there was nothing secret about it. Later he told me that, though the lieutenant had always been talking about his wartime experiences, he never referred to them again after my arrival at the camp.

Many of the students in our room often asked me to tell them about my time in action against the Germans but I hated to talk about the war because so many of my friends had been killed and for me these were sad memories.

Chapter 12: Hard Times in England

In Ludwigsburg we were asked to choose the country where we would like to settle. Radek wanted to go to Canada, but I chose England because it was closer to home; I hoped the *coup* would not last long and I would be able to go back to my family. Another reason was that during my short time in England I had found the people very friendly and kind-hearted.

Soon after Radek left for Canada I moved to Munster, where people were waiting to go to England. A problem arose at my medical examination. During an air raid in France I had been hit in the face by a brick and lost a few of my front teeth. Before I could be accepted for England I had to have them repaired. I had no money, but luckily there was a vacancy in the camp police and as an ex-soldier I got the job. Our duties were to protect the camp against stealing. Two months' wages and the proceeds of selling my suit and shoes raised enough money to get my upper teeth fixed.

I arrived in England in January 1949. I was billeted in an army barracks at West Wratting, near Cambridge, where I made friends with Luboš Novák and Vlastimil Leznar. Vlastík, who spoke English, decided to hitchhike to Manchester to look for work. He was back a week later and told us he had found jobs for us in a weaving factory in a little town named Ramsbottom. As I had no clothes I was given an army uniform dyed navy blue. Our railway tickets were issued and we boarded the train. When we alighted at Ramsbottom Station we were met by a foreman from the factory where we would be working. He was pleasant and friendly, greeting us with a smile – he remained my friend till the end of his life.

We lodged with Miss Burns, an elderly lady, who had two spare rooms. For bed, breakfast and evening meal we paid £2 each but had to buy our own lunch. On Friday, the day after our arrival, we reported to the Police Station and the Labour Exchange to register We were given identity cards before going to see the factory where we would be working and signed an agreement to stay in this employment for one year – this condition we had to accept. If we wanted to change our employment or our address we could do this only with authorisation from the Labour Exchange and the police.

On Sunday we were invited to dinner at the home of Mr. Tom Berry, the man who had met us at the station. We were welcomed warmly into his family. His wife was a lovely lady and they had one daughter. The parents were very pleasant, but I did not care very much for their daughter. She tried to be someone she was not; she wore heavy make-up, smoked like a factory chimney and generally behaved like a spoilt brat. I felt sorry for her parents but realised that they must bear some of the blame for they had let her have all her own way as a child.

When we reported for work on Monday we were told that we would initially be employed as trainee weavers; during this time we would be paid £2.10.0 per week. The English pound had twenty shillings, with twelve pence in each shilling. We were shocked to realise that when we had paid for our lodgings and bought our lunches we would be left with no money. The training period was three months but in two weeks we asked the management to give us our own looms so that we could earn more. We explained that we could not manage on his low wage because we had come with nothing and we needed to buy clothes. I was the worst off, as I did not have a decent suit.

Soon everyone in the mill knew how little we had and our co-workers started bringing in second-hand clothes for us, which, as a tailor, I was able to alter so at least we had clothes for work. The management gave us three looms each to begin with, but soon saw that we were coping very well and gave us more. Within six months I was running eight looms and was earning £7 per week. As we were on piecework I lost money if any of my looms had mechanical problems. Because the tackler was always very busy I often had to wait my turn so I decided to join an evening class at the Technical School to learn how to repair the looms. I knew only a few words of English but learnt by watching our teacher and making notes in Czech; then I would practice on my own looms. I learnt a lot and soon was able to do all my own repairs. Sometimes I helped my neighbours when they had to wait too long for the tackler.

I used to go to the market in nearby Bury, where I could buy remnants of cloth to make trousers and jackets for Luboš, Vlastík and myself so that we could look more respectable. To save money I walked the few miles into town and back. I decided to write to my parents, using another name. The reply brought the sad news that my father had died aged fifty six. I took this news very badly – I felt guilty that I was away when he needed me. He had worked very hard all his life, sometimes doing double shifts so that he could provide a little more for his family, and when he really needed help I was not there. My hatred for Germany and Communism increased; it was because of them I had twice had to leave my home.

My sister wrote that in my absence I had been sentenced to sixteen years imprisonment. My mother, as a widow, received no pension for six months after Father's death, and then only Kr.300 a month, on which it was impossible to live. On top of all this, my brother Ruda had decided to marry but had no money for the wedding. I had saved a little so I bought some black material, which I cut into six pieces of such a size that a tailor could use them to make a suit. I sent these in separate registered envelopes, which they received safely and my brother confirmed that his suit was ready in time for the wedding. He also mentioned that there was no duty to pay on second-hand clothes. When my friends at work realised how difficult the situation was in Czechoslovakia they collected a lot of old clothes, which I sent home to my family. They were very grateful because these were in good condition and they could wear them.

A tackler in the factory was usually paid about £15 a week – double the wage I earned. When a vacancy came up I immediately applied for this. The Director would willingly have given me the job, but the fact that I did not belong to the Trade Union caused a problem. I was willing to become a member if that was the condition of getting the position. The Union, however, turned down my application, telling me that I needed a sponsor before my application could be considered. I found out later that to join the Tacklers' Union was difficult because most of them were related to each other and they liked to keep it that way.

We had now been working in the mill for a year and our initial contract was at an end. I decided to look for other employment; work as a weaver had no future prospects. I was surprised when the management refused to accept my notice, telling me that the contract had been extended to two years and I must work out this time with them. I objected, because I was sure they could not change the terms without my consent.

My leg was still giving me trouble and when I went to the doctor he put me on sick leave. My friend, Vlastík, who understood English well, helped me to write a letter to the Home Office. I complained about the change in my working contract without my consent. I also sent back to them my Military Medal and citation. When this had been presented to me at the British Embassy in Prague I had been told that, if ever I needed assistance, I could go to any British Embassy in the world, where they would do their best to help me. I told them this promise was worthless when, in Britain itself, I was not allowed to change my employment at the end of the one-year contract I had agreed. I received a reply, together with my medal and citation, telling me to take the letter enclosed to my local Labour Exchange, where everything would be regularized.

I went there immediately. The Manager had already been informed and he told me there had been a misunderstanding; I could change my employment at any time and work in any place I wanted.

I decided to go back to tailoring. I had worked only two years before my Jewish employer's business was closed after the German occupation and did not receive my diploma, for which three years training was necessary. I learnt that in England a tailor did not need a certificate as long as he knew how to do the job well. The first place to which I applied for work gave me a waistcoat, already cut out, to make at home; whether they would employ me would depend on the quality of my work. At my lodgings there was no sewing machine but Mrs. Berry let me use hers. I had used it a few times when I had been making clothes for my friends and myself. I did a very good job on that waistcoat and the tailor was pleased with the result. He was particularly interested in the buttonholes and told me he had never seen them made like that. I had done a chain buttonhole, with the thread double-twisted round the needle. It takes longer to make but it looks much better. He offered me employment straight away and I was very happy. The shop was in the centre of Bury, about five kilometres from Ramsbottom, where I was living. I went to work by bus, but later found digs in Bury because I sometimes had to work late at night and found it difficult to catch the last bus home. I soon realised that my boss was not a tailor. He had attended a cutting course in London but had no idea how actually to make a suit. I worked on suits for customers with special requests but most of his suits he sent off to a factory. It didn't take long for me to understand he was using me. Sometimes he told me that a suit I was working on needed to be finished for the next day and I had to work late into the night to finish it on time. Our working hours were 8am to 6pm with half an hour for lunch, though when there was an urgent job to finish I would go in at 6am. In addition I worked every Saturday because we had so much work. The wage for a forty eight hour week was £7 and I was not paid for overtime. Sometimes I worked ninety hours a week. To begin with I did not mind – I was glad to have the job and the business was growing. My employer's behaviour, however, began to change over the next few months. He was coming later to work and gave me the keys so that I could open the shop at 8 o'clock every morning. He was visiting pubs and clubs in the day, as well as in the evening. Often, when a customer came in, I had to telephone around to try to find him, which could take a long time. If a customer could not wait I had to do the fitting. Worst of all was that sometimes at the end of the week I did not receive my wage of £7.

One Saturday afternoon when I called to collect my money the shop was open and he was lying on a table upstairs, drunk. I stayed in the shop until evening and as he had not woken up I locked up and left him there. He apologized on the Monday, telling me that he had not been very well.

I had worked there nearly eighteen months, when one day my boss said he had been robbed of four lengths of material. The shop had not been broken into and only he and I had keys. Although there was one other tailor working there he did not have access to the premises. The missing materials were the most expensive cloths, which meant the thief knew what he was looking for. I immediately handed over my set of keys, and told him that I did not want to have them any longer. He tried to convince me that he did not suspect me but I pointed out that with no evidence of a break in, it had to be someone who had access to the shop. He knew very well where the materials were. A few days later as I was packing some suits, which were cut and ready to send off to a factory for making up, I saw a roll of cloth hidden beneath the wrapping paper in the corner of the storeroom. I remembered that my boss had been discussing the insurance of the shop and stock with another tailor. Because I still did not speak much English they were talking freely and though I could not understand everything I did catch a few words. They had exchanged some materials between themselves and planned to claim against their insurances. This episode upset me so much that I decided that I must move on.

Chapter 13: The Fruits of Honest Labour

I went back to Ramsbottom, where I rented a room over a baker's shop, and began to work for myself. Mr. Berry lent me his treadle sewing machine and stood as guarantor to the bank for £100 so that I could buy some materials and the trimmings I would need. I bought a second-hand table and chairs at an auction and so I was ready to start on my own.

I found it difficult to open accounts as firms with whom I wished to trade were hesitant because I was not a British subject. I solved this by asking an English friend, who was working in a factory, to become my partner and I offered to train him as a tailor. The first week I opened a customer came in with a suit, asking me if I could let it out because he had put on a lot of weight. After examining it I realised I could do nothing because the suit was ready-to-wear and had only narrow seams. He was going to a wedding the following day and this was his only suit; he was too big to buy off the peg and asked if I could make one for him. I could, but only if he chose one of the lengths of cloth I carried in stock. This was at eight o'clock on Friday morning when he was on his way to work. I said I would need to make two fittings – and arranged for him to call during his dinner hour and again after he finished work. I worked all day and all night on that suit without stopping. I ate fruit and drank water because there was no time to make a meal.

I delivered the suit to him at ten o'clock the next morning. He was very nervous because he did not believe I could manage it. When he saw me he was so relieved he nearly hugged me. Being able to make a suit in so short time gave my reputation a big boost. In the speech he gave at the wedding, he told the guests:
"Yesterday this material was on the table, and today I am wearing it. In our small town we've got ourselves a very good tailor and we must keep him here." That was my first week in business.

A patient in hospital recommended me to his doctor, who wanted to wear an overcoat his grandfather had given him, so as not to upset the old man. It was very shabby and he asked if I could do anything to make it look more presentable. I said I could repair it or I could do a first class job by completely renovating the coat. He told me he wanted the best I could do, whatever the cost. When he came to collect it he did not believe that this was his coat. I was shocked, and reminded him that he had asked me to do the best job I could. He assured me that he liked the coat but did not think it was the same garment. With relief, I explained that I had taken the coat to pieces and reversed the cloth. The original was a plain grey Crombie but the reverse had a faint check. The coat looked like a new one. I lifted the lining to show him the reverse, which had originally been on the outside. He was delighted and said his grandfather would be happy to see that he was wearing his overcoat. He told everyone what a good tailor I was, so many new customers were coming to me. I was so busy I could scarcely cope with the work and began looking for more workers. One of these was a Polish boy, Olek, who was working in the mines, but wanted to return to his old trade. I soon realised that there were very few tailors in England. Many shops were sending their suits to be made up in factories, which was cheaper than paying a tailor. I was training Bill Murphy, my new partner, to make trousers and employed a lady who helped with repairs and finishing suits. As I knew I must train staff if I wanted them to work to my standard I decided to take school-leavers as apprentices. I now had six workers and needed more.

    One day I went to party where a couple were celebrating their daughter's birthday, to which a lot of young people were invited. One of them was a young lady for whom I was making a coat - she was my customer No. 26. I liked her very much and after a short conversation I plucked up courage to ask her if she would like to go to the cinema. I was very happy when she accepted and so we started going out together. Sheila worked in Manchester in a travel agency. To begin with we met only on Saturdays as I worked late in the evening and it was after six o'clock when she got home from the city.

After leaving the weaving mill my two friends, Luboš and Vlastík, left for Australia. Vlastík qualified as an accountant in Sydney, where he still lives, and Luboš, an architect, later moved on to San Francisco. I too had applied to go but could not get on a ship; because so many people were emigrating at that time I would have to wait at least a year before I could expect a place. I nearly forgot my request to emigrate until one day I received a letter offering me a passage. It hit me very hard that I could not accept because by this time I had bought materials and some sewing machines on hire purchase. Altogether I owed £500, which I would have to pay before I could leave. I did not have so much money so I decided that I would try to build up my business and apply again later. When I told Sheila what had happened she offered to help me and so we started working together. Sheila, a farmer's daughter, had three brothers and a sister. Every evening she came to see me straight from work and helped me with my correspondence and orders. Once a week on Saturday we went to the local pictures. Many evenings when she was helping me, I would walk her home after we had finished the work, usually around midnight, and when I got back I would carry on working until 3am. I started work again at 6am. It was very hard to get up in the morning but I needed the money to buy materials and to pay my workers. The more orders I got the harder it became. It took six to eight weeks from receiving the order to finishing the suit and getting paid for the job. Sheila helped me where she could and I was very grateful. I wondered how I could repay her. I decided to make her an evening dress and take her to a New Year's Eve dance. The dress was beautiful and everyone admired it. When she told them who made it I was inundated with requests for wedding dresses and evening dresses. Every time I finished an order people would tell their friends and even more customers came to me.

   I started my business in 1951. I had known Sheila eight months when I asked her for her hand in marriage and we were married on 8th January 1953. My friends, Mr. and Mrs. Berry stood in for my parents, which I appreciated very much. I felt that

I was not alone and that I had someone even though they were not blood relations. Our honeymoon was to be three days in Blackpool. We travelled on the bus from Bolton and that evening, Sheila assures me, we saw the film "Von Ryan's Express." We stayed only one night. I was looking forward to a rest but at 6am the following morning we were woken by banging; a plumber was working on the central heating. At 8am, before we were up, the chambermaid wanted to make up the bed and tidy the room.

We decided to go home, where I immediately started work, but the day after that we stayed in bed two hours longer. That was our honeymoon. We had planned to wait at least two years before starting a family so that we could save some money. Sheila was still working in Manchester and one of her friends recommended a supposedly foolproof method of birth control. This advice was not much good because within two months Sheila realised she was pregnant, so we started making plans for the new arrival. Once she had to give up her job, we sorely missed the £8 per week that she earned. We were living in rooms on the top floor, above my workroom, where we had a bedroom and a kitchen; the bathroom and lavatory were on the first floor. Our son, Tony, was born on 25th October, 1953 and we realised that our home was not suitable for bringing up a child. We found a little house with a living room, tiny kitchen and two rooms upstairs at a rent of ten shillings per week. The biggest snag was that the lavatory was outside. We moved in, and used one of the upstairs rooms as a bedroom; the other we divided into two – half a bathroom and the other half a nursery. Later we planned to put a lavatory in the bathroom, but for the time being we had to use the one outside.

The plumber, who was installing our bathroom, asked how much rent I paid for my workroom. When I told him £2.15.0 per week, which was a lot of money for me, he offered to rent me half of his business premises for ten shillings a week. I gladly accepted. This building was on the main road, where I could put out a large board with my name, advertising that I was a tailor.

This was very noticeable, especially from passing buses. It was an excellent position and brought me even more customers.

A few months later, my previous employer's sister-in-law was planning to return to her home in Jamaica. She lived in a large house, consisting of twelve rooms. It had been converted from an old pub but, because the building was in need of renovation, she was unable to sell it. She offered it to me for £600. I did not have the money to buy it but she accepted my offer to pay £20 monthly, so we left our little home. The extra room was very welcome to us as we now had a daughter, Lindsay, born on 13th February, 1955.

One of my customers owned a large factory and lived in a beautiful house; he was a very friendly man, who gave me excellent advice. He himself had started with nothing and told me that, if I were willing to work, I could go far. He told me not to be afraid – there was lots of opportunity in England. When I found a shop for sale in the centre of the town, in an excellent trading spot, even though it was in very bad condition, his advice was to take it; he offered to lend me £200 to do the necessary repairs.

The owner of the premises, a photographer, lived in the Lake District. I had to tell him that, although I would like the property, I did not have the £250 he was asking. I needed what little money I had to repair the property. He agreed that I could pay by instalments of £2.50 per week, free of interest, which, at £10 per month, would make the shop mine in two years. I signed a contract with him, as I did with the friend who was lending me the money for repairs. The latter did not want any interest and told me I could pay him back as and when I could. I promised him that I would make him a suit every year for as long as I was using his money.

I started to renovate my new premises. It had a cellar, two rooms on the ground floor, two big rooms on the first floor and three rooms on the second floor, which apart from the shop area were all used as workrooms. It was located on the square in the centre of the town, so I was gaining new customers all the time.

After the Hungarian Uprising in 1956, many refugees were coming to England. Because we had plenty of room in our house we offered to take in two families. One of these men was a tailor, who came to work for me. He mentioned to his friends that I was looking for workers and three of them asked for employment.

I gave them all accommodation for a reasonable rent and bought for my family a house in Bury, where many of my customers lived. I decided to rent a shop there, next to the railway station, which was in a good position.

A friend who had been an officer in the Czech Army of the West, instead of returning home after the war, had stayed on in England where his wife was a doctor in a local hospital. They had marital problems and were in the process of obtaining a divorce. He had nowhere to stay, so I offered to sell him my big house for the same price I had paid. He could pay me £5 per week, interest free. For him this was a good move because he had tenants paying rent amounting to £15 per week. I also gave him a job as a salesman in the shop; he was, after all, my countryman and I remembered how a man feels when he needs help.

I soon realised how difficult it was to manage two shops but I had a lucky break. One evening Sheila and I were watching "The Three Musketeers" at the Odeon Cinema in Bury. I was startled to hear someone nearby exclaim in Czech: "Jesus Maria!" (This is a typical Czech expression of surprise). At the end of the film I looked around and recognized a girl from Bližanovy, a village near Vojovice, where I had been stationed when we returned home at the end of the war. I tried to catch up with her but lost her in the crowd of people leaving the cinema. I had kept in touch with her cousin, Slavka, whom I knew well, and next day I wrote to her to for Helenka's address.

Helenka was living in Bury with her husband, Karel, and another Czech couple who later moved to Southern Rhodesia. Karel worked as a tailor in Manchester and was happy to take over the management of the business in Bury so I could look after the Ramsbottom branch, where the workroom needed closer supervision. Because I was spending so much time in the other shop the workers were becoming slack and I needed to spend more time with them.

When our third child, Peter, was born on 2nd January, 1958 we had just moved to our new house in Bury. We were happy there but I lost a lot of time travelling. I often had to work late and was very tired by the time I got home. Behind the shop in Ramsbottom was a small house, which I demolished and replaced with a two-storey building, the ground floor becoming the shop, with a large workroom above it. In the original building I opened a department selling ready-to-wear suits and converted the upper floors into a flat. We had a large living room and kitchen/diner and upstairs three bedrooms and a bathroom. I opened the passage through from the old to the new shop so that it was easy to get to and from our living quarters.

As soon as we had sold our house in Bury we moved into this flat. This cut out the time and expense of travelling and we started saving for a family home with a garden. We had more and more work, which kept us busy all the time. I employed twenty five people of different nationalities – Czech, Slovak, Hungarian, Italian, Spanish and French. I took English people only as apprentices, whom I trained to my standards and they all became very good tailors.

Chapter 14: Back Home after 20 years

I was in touch by letter with my family, who wrote that the situation in the Republic was changing and it was now possible that they could come to visit me. To enable them to do this I must send an official invitation, authenticated by a solicitor. In 1967 the first to come was my sister, Marie, accompanied by her ten-year-old son, Pavel. She liked it here and, when I asked her if there was any place she would particularly like to see, she had only one wish – to go to a supermarket. She had never seen so much food and other goods in one place; she told us that at home in Těšin the shops were empty. Anything beyond the basics could only be bought on the black market, which was very expensive and beyond their means. I had taken British nationality a few years earlier. She told me that, even though I had been sentenced to sixteen years' jail when I left home nineteen years before, these convictions were now cancelled. In 1968, after twenty years of exile, I applied to relinquish my Czech nationality and this was granted. I was now able to ask for a tourist visa so that I could take my family to visit my homeland. This was the year of the Prague Spring, when, twenty years after the Communist coup, Dubček tried to introduce "Communism with a human face."

In July we set off by car, all travelling on British passports. In our luggage I had a lot of presents for my family – something for everyone, though I was worried that they might be confiscated when we came to the Czech border. We crossed into Czechoslovakia at Mikulov near Vienna. It was a strange feeling; I was coming home after twenty years and did not know what would be waiting for me. Crossing the border in those days was not a pleasant welcome for a fellow countryman; it was a frightening experience, especially for Sheila and the children. I was telling myself that I was an idiot and wondering whether they would let us out again. I was worrying about what kind of situation I had got us into as we drove northwards. Suddenly, as we were passing through a village, I was startled by an ear-splitting noise. I stopped, shocked, wondering what was happening. Music was blasting from loudspeakers hanging on poles throughout the village. A few minutes later a voice announced: "Comrade Number so-and-so, report to area number so-and-so."

Because Sheila and the children did not speak Czech they thought we had done something wrong. In the beginning I too thought I had broken some regulation but later learnt that this was the norm in villages where there were collective farms. The workers were shifted from one workplace to another by broadcast instructions.

The roads were in a very bad state of repair. We were constantly sent on diversions through small villages, where conditions looked very poor. The plaster was falling off the houses, everything looked shabby and neglected. When I asked directions from some villagers they were afraid to talk to me. They pointed out the road I should take and quickly moved away.

We finally reached my hometown. When I looked towards the Beskydy Mountains, where I had spent so many happy hours in my youth, I was very emotional. The memories came flooding back. I remembered my weekends there as a young boy, my first Scout Camp and after the formation of our own Mosty troop, singing with visitors from Prague and Brno on Velký Polom. There were also less happy memories of those weekends, before the Germans placed the mountains out of bounds, when my friends and I were trying to work out a way to escape the Nazi occupation.

In Těšin we stayed with my elder brother, Leoš. On our first evening, to toast my return, Sheila was offered a typical Czech drink, slivovic (plum brandy), but opted for a raspberry drink. The only thing she did not realise was that there were about three drops of raspberry juice in a glassful of neat schnapps. She cannot remember very much about that evening. The whole family got together at my sister's house in the village of Mosty, which had been the family home before I had left for the West. The house was badly in need of repair but materials were scarce and when they were available they were too expensive for them to buy. It was good to meet them all and, when I gave each one the present I had brought, such happiness I have never seen.

The next day I had to report to the police. I was warned not to get into conversation with anyone, as no one could be trusted. Leoš went with me to the County Police Headquarters in Karvina so that I would not need to ask for directions. When we arrived there was a long queue. I was glad he was with me – he told me that these were people applying for visas to go abroad. He led me into another office where about ten people were waiting and advised me to hold my British passport in my hand so that the clerk could see it. Before we left home he had also told me that it would be a good idea to take a packet of English cigarettes and to offer one to the clerk when I was called into the office. To my surprise everything happened as he had predicted. A female clerk appeared, saw my passport and led me into her office. She noted our passport details, asking me where I was staying and for how long. She was curious to know how people were living in England. I was very careful in my reply. I told her I had a tailoring business and that one had to work hard wherever one was. I noticed the ashtray on her desk and offered her a cigarette. At first she declined but when she saw the brand name she agreed to try one, as she had never smoked an English cigarette. Because the packet was still sealed I said she could keep it as I had more for my own use. She was very grateful and put them in her desk drawer, telling me she would smoke them later. I was surprised when she said I need not report back to her before I left; she would complete everything there and then. I was grateful, as this would save another day of my holiday. She stamped the passports and visas and wished me a happy stay in Czechoslovakia. When I told Leoš what had happened he explained that everyone would accept English cigarettes; they were unavailable in the Republic and on the black market they were very expensive.

I spent the next two weeks with my family. When we all got together the youngsters would sometimes make a campfire around which we would sit, eating sausages roasted on sticks. Afterwards we would sing the old songs until the fire was out.

There would be crazy games of hide and seek, and the adults enjoyed these as much as the young ones. Our children loved playing in the woods next to the house; they were there all day. Though none of them spoke the language they were soon able to communicate with their cousins – a few words of English, a few of Czech and a lot of hand-signals did the trick.

To save their clothes, I decided to buy them tracksuits but when I went into Těšin I soon found there were none to be had. At one shop I was told they might have some the next day. My sister offered to get them for me because to be near the head of the queue she would need to be there by 6am. Whenever there was a new delivery there was always a great demand. I was glad I did not need to get up so early. Marie waited from 6am to 10am and finally managed to get one tracksuit. This was too small to fit any of my children. Each person could buy only one item and was not allowed to choose the size. Customers exchanged the clothes between themselves in the street outside the shop. She had tried all over town but there were no more tracksuits available.

One day we went to visit my beloved Beskydy. We drove out to the foot of the mountains and took the chairlift to the top of Javorovy. The kids loved the lift, especially at the beginning of the descent where the chair always did a mini wobbly and they suddenly realised that it was a long, long way down to the tops of the very tall pine trees below them.

The day before we were due to leave Marie was unable to find any salami for sandwiches, but she had heard that there might be a delivery the next morning. Again she was standing in a queue at 6am, but at 10am was disappointed to learn that no salami had been delivered. I told her to stop worrying about us. We would soon be in Austria where we could buy food easily. It was very sad to see how the people had to cope with all these shortages.

That summer the political situation between the Czech and Russian leaders was extremely tense. Dubček was under intense pressure; his dream of "Communism with a human face" was not popular with other member states in the Eastern bloc. Sheila was unaware of what was happening, though rather surprised that whenever she saw a television the programme was about politics. We arrived home on August 21st and heard that the armies of five Warsaw Pact states had invaded my country, bringing the "Prague Spring" to an end.

After this, we returned to Czechoslovakia a few times, although there were years when I was refused a visitor's visa, the reason for which I never discovered. On these later visits we crossed the border from Germany at Rozvadov. Sheila always liked this route as it led through the town of Bor, where we always passed a prominent landmark she thought of as Rapunzel's tower. The border control on the German side was just a hand-operated barrier through which we passed quickly; on the Czech side things were very different. There was a huge mechanized steel barrier, where we would have to wait for at least an hour and a half, during which time we were not allowed to leave the car. Above us was a watchtower, from where a guard with a machine gun could see everything that was going on and outside armed soldiers with dogs patrolled constantly. Sheila and the children were very nervous. At last they would let us through but we could wait another two or three hours before a border guard came to check our passports and visas. Once I was informed that the visas were not valid because I had written the registration number of the car only on my own visa when it should have been on all five. I apologized and was ready to fill in this information but the guard took them from me and said he would do it. He told me I must change currency; it was obligatory at that time for visitors to buy a certain amount of Czech crowns per person per day. For us this came to £300, which was quite a lot in those days. We received eighteen crowns per pound sterling. When we reached our destination we learnt that the going rate on the black market was one hundred and twenty crowns per pound.

Finally we would be allowed through but were forbidden to stop until we had passed the second barrier about a kilometre further on, where, once again, our papers would be checked.

To help my family I usually brought them clothes or dress materials they could not get in the shops. They were always grateful and appreciated anything I could bring.

Chapter 15: At Home in England

We wanted to give our children the best education possible. Tony went to a private school and Lindsay to the Convent Junior School. When the fees for Tony's school doubled we realised that we would not be able to afford these for three children, so he finished his education at a local grammar school. After finishing her secondary education at Bury Convent, Lindsay went on to University. Peter attended a private secondary school but he was never academic, did not want to study and left school when he was sixteen.

I converted two rooms on the ground floor into a shop for Peter to run – we called it Moravian Fried Chicken, where they sold chicken, chips and salads. He was running this well, working from lunchtime to midnight. Because of his late finish I bought him a motorbike so he could get home easily. We had by then moved to a house in Holcombe Brook, where we had more room and a garden.

Two years later Peter had an accident when a car entering the main road collided with his motorbike. He was in hospital for about four months so we had to run the chicken shop as well as my tailoring business. There was no one else to take over so, eventually, we had to close it. About this time we also closed our tailoring outlets in Manchester and Bury.

When we received and accepted an offer of £20,000 for the whole building, we bought a shop in a better spot across the square for £7,500. We had to do some refurbishment, but it was in a prominent position on the main road and anyone stopping at the traffic lights could not fail to notice us.

Tony had left school and started work in a bank; Lindsay had finished at university and was looking for a job. She worked in a hotel until she got a post with Laker Airlines at Gatwick Airport. She was good at her job and later transferred to Manchester Airport, where she was in charge of the Laker office. Unfortunately this company went into liquidation but we saw a small advertisement for a travel firm needing temporary staff in

Switzerland. She moved there and worked on a seasonal basis. She returned to England between seasons, before being employed by her company on a permanent full time basis and becoming a Swiss resident.

After the accident Peter could not stand for long periods. I offered him a job and he is now running the family firm. He had a good head for business and we opened shops in Great Harwood, Horwich, Nelson and later Rawtenstall. When he married he lived in a flat above the Ramsbottom shop, later buying a house about a mile away.

The housing market was favourable when we sold our house in Holcombe Brook and moved to a bungalow in Ramsbottom, where we lived for ten years. A friend who had always liked our home bought it from us; house values had risen so much that I made a reasonable profit and moved to a house just round the corner from Peter.

When I was sixty-five my wife and I went round the world via America, Hawaii, Fiji, New Zealand and Australia, where we spent some time in New South Wales and Victoria with Sheila's brother and my old friend, Vlastík, with whom we visited a Sokol festival in Sydney. From Australia we flew to Singapore for a few days, before returning home. This was a memorable experience. At the same time I handed over the running of the business to Peter who is still in charge. As well as the retail shops, we started a formal hire business which grew into a large concern. Now we supply shops all over the United Kingdom. We have two factories, 12 vans and in peak season employ 300 people. We sold off our retail outlets when arthritis in my hands made it difficult for me to carry on with the tailoring side of the business.

Although I thought I had retired, I find myself still working for the company. I help whenever and wherever required, and am always on call as a consultant, so I still spend most of my time in the business. Sheila works on the computer, mostly setting up and checking data bases.

Chapter 16: The Joy of 1989

In 1989 came the Velvet Revolution, when my homeland finally threw off the Communist yoke. I was happy that my countrymen were at last free, but sad that at my age I would not be able to enjoy this freedom so much. I travel there often. I still love Silesia which was my home and which I can never forget.

Since this time the Czech Government has treated us old soldiers very well; it is trying to make amends for the wrongs done by the Communists. My Czech citizenship was returned and I was given the honorary rank of Colonel. Since 1995 the Legionnaires have been invited to visit the Republic in June each year, as guests of the Czech Army, who always make us very welcome and ensure that we have an interesting and educational programme.

The year 2003 was for me especially important. I was 80 years old and we spent three months in Australia and the South Pacific. In January we celebrated our Golden Wedding twice, firstly dining out on the Restaurant Tram in Melbourne with our nephew and his wife, and then, because of gaining an extra day as we crossed the date line, in Roratonga in the Cook Islands.

Tony fell in love with a very nice young lady and moved to the Czech Republic; her parents have accepted him into their family circle and I am glad to see how happily they live. Lindsay still enjoys living in Switzerland. She comes home for a few days whenever she can and we telephone each other once or twice a week. Peter, who hopes to retire at a younger age than I shall, is training his children, Clare and Andrew, to run the business, which they want to keep in the family.

I still love my homeland and remember with pleasure my time spent there as a boy. I hope my countrymen in the Czech Republic will protect their freedom and not forget how many young men gave their lives so they could live in a freer world.

Ex-servicemen living in England still keep in touch with each other. We meet several times a year but our numbers are dwindling. Because of this, our twice yearly re-unions, for Czechs living in the North West, has been cut to one held in the Spring. The beseda we used to hold for our National Day on 28th October was abandoned because travel for us older ones is more difficult when the days are getting shorter.

At the beginning of July every year we meet in Cholmondeley Park, near Chester, where the Czechoslovak Army in Exile was formed in 1940. There we have a memorial, with an inscription in Czech, Slovak and English:

> *In Memory of our Comrades*
> *Who gave their lives for the*
> *Freedom of their country.*
> *We will remember them.*

On this occasion we always sing our National Anthem, "Kde domuv můj?" ("Where is my home?")

Our eyes mist as we look into the distance. When we sing these words I hear the sad voices of my comrades and wonder if they have the same thoughts as I have – where really **is** our home?

When I was a little boy we learnt in school that Blaník is a mountain where Czech knights sleep. According to the legend they wake up and come forth to help the Czech homeland whenever danger threatens. When I think of this legend I come to the conclusion that Blaník is the true heart of our Czech country and these knights are patriots who wake up when they realise that the homeland is in peril and hurry to protect it. This has happened several times in the past.

I often visit my country, where everything is changing for the better. There is still much to be done and they still need help. All the time I lived in exile I hoped to return home but I have decided I would try to help them from here in England, where I have more opportunity.

I have been a member of Rotary for forty years. This is an association of businessmen, whose aim is to help those in need. My club, Ramsbottom, undertook to support the Domino orphanage in Plzen and the Club Korálky for mentally and physically handicapped children in Rokycany. With the help of our local Rotaract and Interact Clubs, we support them financially, collect clothes and toys for them and donate Christmas presents, all of which I take out to them twice yearly.

In England, I speak to different organizations about the beauty of the Czech Republic – the mountains, cities, spas, castles and stately homes. The country is steeped in history and everywhere there is something of interest. Because Rotary is an organization of business people I also speak to them of the business opportunities in the Republic. Our family firm, under the direction of my son, Peter, has done business with the Czech Republic since 1989. I am glad that I can make a small contribution to help my countrymen.

In my eighties I have only one wish – that after my death my ashes be laid to rest in my beloved Těšinsko, my home.

APPENDIX: JOSEF NOVÁK

Born 11th March 1923
Army cover name: Jaroslav Bílý
Demobbed   July 1946, Sergeant
Decorations: Military Medal (British)
Citation
Private Jaroslav Bílý (Josef Novák)
During an offensive action
on 5th November 1944
Private Bílý observed heavy mortar fire
concentrated on his own unit.
With another man he stalked the enemy mortar
position with complete disregard for his own
safety and forced the surrender of the entire
enemy mortar platoon, together with the
officer commanding.
This was a fine example of great coolness and
tactical skill.

Medal for Bravery 5th December 1944
Medal for Bravery 14th February 1945
Czech Army Memorial Medal 15th March 1945
Czechoslovak War Cross 1939 13th April 1946
British Campaign Medals: 1939-1945
  France & Germany
  Victory Medal
Czech Campaign Medal: 1939-45
  Czechoslovak Legionnaires
  Commemorative Medal

Member of SOKOL aged 14

Josef Novák in Czechoslovak Army uniform

Josef (left) and his brother Ruda

**Four Czechosloak soldiers from Silesia
(Josef is second from left)**